SPEAK UP!
IT'S YOUR LIFE

— If It Matters to You, It Matters —

Sue Levine
LCSW NBC-HWC

Speak Up! It's Your Life: If It Matters to You, It Matters

By: Sue Levine, LCSW, NBC-HWC

ISBN for Print: 979-8-9990528-0-3

Copyright © 2025, Sue Levine

All rights reserved. No portion of this book may be reproduced in any form without permission from the author, except as permitted by U.S. copyright law.

For permissions, contact: info@suelevine.com

Cover & interior design: Rhianon Paige
Cover art: Thomas Gonzalez

Published by: AFGO Press

Printed in the United States

First Edition 2025

The information in this book is provided for educational and informational purposes only and is not intended as a substitute for professional advice or support. The author is a Licensed Clinical Social Worker and National Board Certified Health and Wellness Coach; however, this book is not intended to serve as therapy or a professional consultation.

Every effort has been made to ensure the accuracy of the content at the time of publication. Readers are encouraged to use their own judgment and seek appropriate guidance from qualified professionals for their individual needs and circumstances.

The experiences and stories shared in this book are either based on the author's personal experiences or are composites created to illustrate key themes. Any resemblance to actual persons, living or dead, is purely coincidental unless explicitly stated.
The author and publisher disclaim any liability or loss incurred directly or indirectly from the use or application of any of the contents of this book.

To women who have stayed silent for too long. May these pages remind you that your voice matters.

TABLE OF CONTENTS

Before We Begin... —————————————————— i

Introduction: "I'm Sorry, Your Father Is Dead" ———— 1

Step 1: Look Within (And Turn Up the Volume) ———— 15

Step 2: Own Your Voice (Shine A Spotlight) ————— 31

Step 3: Understand Your Power (Take the Wheel) ——— 49

Step 4: Decide to Act (From Silence to Inspired Action) – 67

New Adventures in Speaking My Truth ——————— 81

About the Author ———————————————— 97

Acknowledgments ———————————————— 101

Is It Time to Find Your Voice? ——————————

BEFORE WE BEGIN...

Dear Reader,

If you've ever swallowed your words to keep the peace, second-guessed yourself in the moment, or walked away thinking, *I should have said something*, this book is for you.

If you've ever laughed along when something didn't sit right, apologized just to ease the tension—even when you weren't wrong—or stayed quiet in a meeting (even though you had something valuable to say), this book is for you. If you've nodded in agreement while something inside you whispered *no*, downplayed your needs to avoid being "difficult," or kept your thoughts to yourself because speaking up felt too risky—this book is for you, too.

I didn't write this to offer advice or instruction. I wrote it to tell the truth—my own, and maybe yours, too. Like many women, I've spent years navigating situations where silence felt safer than honesty; being agreeable seemed more acceptable than being authentic. I know what it feels like to be dismissed, overlooked, or punished for simply naming what's not working. I also know how powerful it is to reclaim your voice.

This book isn't about blame or easy solutions. It's about awareness—about uncovering the subtle ways we've been conditioned to stay quiet and compliant, and about what happens when we finally begin to speak, even if our voice shakes. It's about choosing to see yourself clearly, to stop waiting for permission, and to start standing firm in what you know to be true.

That said, this book is not a call to speak at all costs. Some women live in situations—such as unsafe home environments or within cultural or community contexts—where speaking up may carry real consequences. If you are in a place where silence is necessary for your safety or survival, then silence is not weakness—*it's wisdom*. Only you can know what's safe, and nothing in these pages is meant to suggest otherwise.

Through these pages, I hope you find not just stories, but a mirror—a way to see yourself more clearly and honestly. You don't have to stay silent any longer. The journey from silence to voice is not a straight line. But it is a path worth walking. One word, one step, one brave moment at a time.

I'm always open to meaningful conversations and thoughtful collaborations. If this book sparks something you'd like to talk about, feel free to reach out to me at info@suelevine.com.

Here's to your brave voice!

Sue Levine, LCSW, NBC-HWC
August 2025

INTRODUCTION

"I'm Sorry, Your Father Is Dead"

I felt that familiar emptiness and loneliness wash over me—helpless, powerless, and afraid. My sense of self-worth vanished, leaving me disconnected and questioning my very existence.

A few years earlier, when I was 15, my mother and I had just returned from an uneventful Labor Day weekend trip to a cooler part of the state to find two policemen waiting at our doorstep. I was approached by one of the officers and taken aside. "I'm so sorry—your father was found dead in his parked car." My father was the one person who truly listened to me, who made space for my voice. With him gone, I felt numb—I felt I had no voice, and that was the day I became invisible.

Growing up, I was surrounded by pessimism, darkness, and negativity. It's hard to shake this off as it feels like it's the core of who I am. For years, I felt invisible and unheard, blending into the background. It took years and many wake-ups before I had a real handle on my own voice and how to use it again.

Sue Levine, LCSW, NBC-HWC

The Moment That Changes Everything

It happens in an instant—that split second when you know you should speak up but don't. Maybe it's when your colleague takes credit for your idea in a meeting, and you sit there silently while your stomach churns. Maybe it's when a family member makes a comment that cuts deep, and you smile politely while your heart pounds. Maybe it's when you witness something that goes against your values, and you walk away knowing you could have made a difference but chose silence instead.

We've all been there. That moment when our authentic self screams to be heard, but we swallow our words and retreat into the familiar safety of silence. Later, we replay the scene in our minds, crafting the perfect response we wish we'd given. We promise ourselves we'll speak up next time. But when the next time comes, we often find ourselves in the same pattern—watching our voice disappear just when we need it most.

If you've picked up this book, chances are you've experienced this disconnect between who you are inside and how you show up in the world. You know you have something valuable to say, but somewhere between your heart and your mouth, your voice gets lost. You're tired of walking away from important moments feeling disappointed in yourself. You're ready to bridge the gap between your inner truth and your outer expression.

This book isn't about teaching you to be someone you're not. It's about helping you remember who you already are underneath the layers of conditioning, fear, and people-pleasing that may have accumulated over the years. Finding your voice isn't about learning to speak—it's about remembering the power and worth of what you have to say.

Why This Matters Now More Than Ever

We live in a time when authentic voices are desperately needed. In our families, workplaces, and communities, we're surrounded by conversations that stay on the surface while the real issues go unaddressed. We're living through an epidemic of silence where people bite their tongues to keep the peace, avoid difficult conversations to maintain comfort, and sacrifice their truth to preserve relationships that often aren't serving anyone well.

This silence comes at an enormous cost. When we don't speak up about things that matter to us, we don't just lose the opportunity to create change—we lose pieces of ourselves. Every time we swallow our words, we send ourselves the message that our thoughts, feelings, and perspectives aren't valuable enough to risk discomfort. Over time, this pattern erodes our confidence, diminishes our sense of agency, and disconnects us from our authentic selves.

The cost isn't just personal—it's collective. When authentic voices remain silent, toxic behaviors go unchecked, inequities persist, and opportunities for growth and connection are lost. The ideas that could solve problems never get shared. The perspectives that could bridge divides never get heard. The truth that could set people free never gets spoken.

But here's what I've learned in my decades of working with people in some of the most challenging circumstances—from psychiatric hospitals to prisons to mediation rooms: Everyone has a voice worth hearing. Everyone has something valuable to contribute. Everyone has the capacity to speak their truth with both courage and compassion. The question isn't whether you have a voice—it's whether you're willing to remember how to use it.

My Journey to Understanding Voice

My own relationship with voice has been forged in the crucible of real human experience. I've spent my career in places where finding your voice isn't optional—it's essential for survival, healing, and hope. In the locked units of one of the country's busiest psychiatric hospitals, I learned that voice is often the last thing we lose and the first thing we need to reclaim. Working with patients experiencing acute psychosis, I witnessed the profound courage it takes to speak your truth when the world seems to be telling you that your reality doesn't matter.

In prison settings, facilitating therapy groups for inmates with serious mental illness, I saw how silence can become both a protection and a prison. These men and women had often learned that speaking up led to punishment, rejection, or worse. Yet in the safety of our group sessions, I watched voices emerge that had been buried for years—voices filled with wisdom, pain, hope, and an unmistakable hunger for authentic connection.

My transition into education brought new insights about voice development. As a Teacher-Librarian, I had the privilege of creating spaces where young people could discover and express their authentic selves. I learned that finding your voice isn't just about speaking up in conflict—it's about knowing who you are, understanding what you value, and having the courage to express that truth in a world that often rewards conformity over authenticity.

Through my training as a mediator in civil and domestic relations, I've seen what happens when people finally find the courage to speak their truth in the midst of conflict. I've witnessed the transformative power of authentic communication and the healing that becomes possible when people stop performing and start being real with each other.

Each of these experiences has taught me something that centers on: Voice isn't about volume, aggression, or domination. It's about presence, authenticity, and the courage to show up as yourself in a world that's constantly inviting you (or pressuring you) to be someone else. It's about finding the intersection between honoring your truth and honoring your relationships. It's about learning to speak up in real time, in the moments when it matters most.

What You Won't Find in This Book

Before we go further, let me be clear about what this book is not. This isn't a collection of clever comebacks or assertiveness scripts that you can memorize and deploy in difficult situations. You won't find generic communication formulas or one-size-fits-all approaches to handling conflict. This isn't about learning to be more aggressive, louder, or more confrontational. It's not strictly a method, although I've studied a few formal approaches over the years.

This book also isn't about blaming others for your silence or positioning yourself as a victim of circumstances beyond your control. While we'll certainly explore how past experiences and cultural conditioning contribute to voice suppression, the focus here is on reclaiming your agency and taking responsibility for how you show up in your own life.

You won't find encouragement to speak up about everything that bothers you or to turn every interaction into an opportunity for self-expression. This isn't about becoming someone who can't let anything slide or who feels compelled to voice every opinion. Wisdom includes knowing when to speak and when to remain silent, and we'll explore that discernment throughout this journey.

Most importantly, this isn't a quick fix or a superficial makeover. Finding your voice is inner work that requires honesty, courage, and patience with yourself. It's about fundamental transformation, not cosmetic changes. The process may challenge you, but it will also liberate you in ways you may not have thought possible.

What You Will Discover

What you will find in these pages is a roadmap for remembering who you are and expressing that truth with both courage and compassion. This book is based on a simple but powerful framework that I've seen transform countless lives: the journey from silence to authentic expression happens in predictable stages, and when you understand and honor those stages, lasting change becomes not just possible but inevitable.

We'll begin by exploring the epidemic of silence that surrounds us—understanding why so many intelligent, capable, caring people struggle to speak up when it matters most. You'll discover the psychological, cultural, and personal factors that contribute to voice suppression, and you'll begin to see your own patterns with clarity and compassion rather than judgment.

Next, we'll dive deep into the psychology of speaking up,

exploring the neurological and emotional processes that happen when we encounter situations that trigger our silence. You'll learn why the fight, flight, or freeze response often overrides our desire to speak up, and how to work with your nervous system rather than against it.

The heart of this book lies in what I call the LOUD (Love) framework—a four-step process for moving from silence to authentic expression:

L - Look Within (And Turn Up the Volume): Before you can speak your truth, you have to know what your truth is. This section will guide you through the process of self-discovery, helping you identify your values, recognize your patterns, and reconnect with the authentic self that may have gotten buried under years of conditioning and compromise. You Turn Up the Volume on your inner voice to hear it above the noise.

O - Own Your Voice (Shine A Spotlight): Once you've reconnected with your authentic self, you need to claim ownership of your right to express that truth. This isn't about arrogance or entitlement—it's about recognizing the inherent worth of your perspective and accepting it fully, in ways that honor both yourself and others.

U - Understand Your Power (Take the Wheel): True voice development requires you to take full responsibility for your responses and choices. You'll learn to move from the passenger seat to the driver's seat of your own life, understanding that while you can't control others, you have complete control over your own actions.

D - Decide to Act (Inspired Action): The final stage involves translating inner alignment into outer expression. You'll discover the difference between forced action and inspired action, and learn to speak up in ways that feel natural and sustainable rather than performed and exhausting.

The (Love) part is that it comes from a decision to love yourself, and your life, and the people around you enough to be honest and forthright and respectful. The reason my process works, as you will come to understand, is because it starts on the inside, where your mind, body, and heart intersect.

Finding your voice is inextricably linked to finding yourself. If you learn to use your voice, it gives you strong feedback and direction about who you really are. And as you grow into yourself, you will find it easier and automatic to speak from your true voice.

When a woman finds her SELF she finds her voice

Throughout this journey, you'll find practical exercises, real-world examples, and strategies for applying these concepts in your daily life. You'll learn specific techniques for managing anxiety, handling difficult conversations, and maintaining your authentic voice even in challenging circumstances.

Who This Book Is For

This book is written for anyone who has ever felt the frustration of knowing they should speak up but finding themselves unable to do so in the moment. It's for the person who replays conversations in their mind, wishing they'd said something else, maybe *anything* else. It's for the individual who has important things to say but struggles to find their voice when it matters.

You might be someone who speaks up easily in some situations but freezes in others. Maybe you're comfortable advocating for others but struggle to advocate for yourself. Perhaps you find your voice in writing but lose it in face-to-face conversations. Or you might be someone who has been silent, stifled, or settling for so long that you're not even sure what your authentic voice *sounds like* anymore.

This book is particularly relevant for women, who are often socialized to prioritize others' comfort over their own truth, but these principles will apply to anyone who has learned that being agreeable is more important than being authentic. It's for people in helping professions who give so much to others that they forget to advocate for themselves. It's for individuals in organizational cultures that discourage dissent or questioning of authority.

If you're tired of feeling powerless in your own life, ready to stop abandoning yourself in favor of keeping others comfortable, and committed to becoming someone who can speak their truth with both courage and compassion, then this book is for you.

What Makes This Approach Different

Most approaches to assertiveness and communication focus on techniques and scripts—what to say and how to say it. While these elements have their place, they miss the fundamental truth that sustainable voice development must begin from the inside out. You can learn all the communication strategies in the world, but if you haven't done the inner work of understanding who you are and what you stand for, those techniques will feel foreign and be difficult to sustain.

This book takes a different approach. Instead of starting with external behaviors, we begin with internal awareness. Instead of trying to teach you to become someone different, we focus on helping you become more fully yourself. Instead of providing scripts to memorize, we help you connect with your authentic voice so that your words flow naturally from who you really are.

The framework presented here is also unique in its integration of psychological insight with practical application. Drawing from my background in clinical social work, education, mediation, wellness, and personal coaching, this approach addresses both the emotional and practical aspects of voice development. You'll understand not just what to do, but why certain patterns exist and how to transform them at their root.

Perhaps most importantly, this approach recognizes that finding your voice isn't a destination—it's a practice. It's not something you achieve once and then possess forever. It's a dynamic, evolving process of staying connected to your authentic self and expressing that truth in an ever-changing world. The goal isn't perfection: it's presence, authenticity, and the courage to keep showing up as yourself.

The Promise of This Journey

I can't promise that this journey will be easy or that you'll never struggle with self-expression again. What I can promise is that if you're willing to do the work—the real, honest, sometimes uncomfortable work of looking within and owning your truth—you will experience a transformation that goes far beyond your communication skills.

You'll discover that finding your voice isn't just about speaking up in difficult situations, though you'll certainly develop that capacity. It's about living with greater authenticity, building more genuine relationships, and creating a life that truly reflects who you are rather than who others expect you to be.

You'll learn that your voice is not a luxury or an indulgence—it's an essential part of your humanity that deserves to be honored and expressed. You'll understand that speaking your truth isn't selfish—it's a gift to others who are also longing for more authentic connection and communication.

Most importantly, you'll remember something you may have forgotten: you already have everything you need to find your voice. You don't need to become someone different or develop abilities you don't possess. You need to remember who you've always been underneath the conditioning and fear, and find the courage to express that truth in the world.

How to Use This Book

This book is designed to be both read and experienced. While you can certainly read it straight through to understand the concepts, the real transformation happens when you engage with the exercises, reflect on the questions, and begin applying the principles in your daily life.

I encourage you to read with a journal nearby. The insights that emerge as you work through this material are valuable and worth capturing. Pay attention to what resonates with you and what triggers resistance—both responses contain important information about your journey.

The chapters build on each other, so I recommend working through them in order rather than jumping around. Each section prepares you for the next, and skipping ahead may leave you without the foundation you need for later concepts.

Most importantly, be patient and compassionate with yourself as you work through this material. Finding your voice is a process, not an event. There will be moments of breakthrough and moments of setback. There will be times when you feel confident and times when you feel uncertain. All of this is normal and part of the journey.

Remember that you're not trying to become someone you're not—you're trying to become more fully who you already are. Your authentic voice is not something you need to create; it's something you need to remember and honor. It's been with you all along, waiting for you to come home to it.

Your Voice Matters

As we begin this journey together, I want you to know something that you may have forgotten or never fully believed: Your voice matters. Not because of your credentials, accomplishments, or social status, but because you are a unique human being with a perspective that no one else possesses. Your experiences, insights, and truth have value, and the world needs what you have to offer.

The silence epidemic that surrounds us isn't just about individual people failing to speak up—it's about a collective forgetting of how much each voice matters. We've become so focused on not offending, not disrupting, not making waves, we've forgotten the creative, healing, transformative power of true expression.

But transformation is possible, both for individuals and for our communities. Every time someone finds the courage to speak their truth with compassion, they create permission for others to do the same. Every time someone chooses authenticity over people-pleasing, they model a different way of being in the world. Every time someone stands up in real time for what they believe in, they contribute to a culture where authentic voices are valued and heard.

Your journey toward finding your voice isn't just personal—it's part of a larger movement toward more authentic, honest, and compassionate communication. As you learn to speak your truth, you're not just changing your own life; you're contributing to a world where everyone's voice can be heard and valued. Isn't that something we can all believe in?

Your voice is waiting for you to remember its power and use it in service of what matters most to you. The question isn't whether you have something valuable to say—it's whether you're ready to say it.

Let's begin.

STEP 1: LOOK WITHIN

(And Turn Up the Volume)

I was sitting in my graduate research seminar when the discussion turned to research methodologies—a topic I had spent weeks diving into. I had solid insights and thoughtful questions that could have deepened the conversation, but as soon as I considered speaking up, something familiar happened: My heart started to race, my throat tightened, and the words dissolved.

I looked around the room at faces that seemed so confident, so certain, and I made the same choice I'd made countless times before—I stayed silent. Part of the reason was the memory of the last time I spoke in class: a couple of classmates smirked, and the professor moved on from my comment without any acknowledgement. I felt dismissed—like what I had to say didn't matter. I didn't want to risk that feeling again.

Later that day, I found myself replaying the class meeting over and over. What would have happened if I had spoken up? Would they have listened? Would they have dismissed me?

The questions swirled, but underneath them was a deeper, more unsettling realization: I had been disappearing, piece by piece, meeting by meeting, conversation by conversation. Somewhere along the way, I had learned that my voice was optional, that my insights were secondary, that keeping the peace was more important than speaking my truth.

This wasn't the first time. As I began to pay attention, I realized it was happening everywhere. With my family, when I'd nod along with dinner plans I didn't want. With friends, I'd laugh at comments that made me uncomfortable. With colleagues, I'd absorb extra work rather than say no. I had become an expert at reading the room and adjusting myself accordingly, but I had forgotten how to read *myself*.

The loss of my voice hadn't happened overnight. It had been a gradual erosion, so subtle that I didn't notice it happening. Like a river slowly carving through rock, years of small compromises had worn away something essential. I had become so skilled at anticipating what others wanted to hear that I had stopped listening to what I needed to say.

The Invisible Prison of Unawareness

I struggled with this pattern for so long because I wasn't even aware of how often I kept silent or how deeply ingrained it had become. I've learned that awareness is the first and most essential step in reclaiming your voice. You can't change what you don't see. And for years, my silence was so automatic—so embedded in my everyday interactions—that it simply felt normal.

This lack of awareness wasn't just about the obvious moments—the times when I should have spoken up in meetings or pushed back against unreasonable requests. It was more insidious than that. It was the way I would edit my thoughts before speaking, softening my language to make it more palatable. It was the way I would defer to others' expertise even in areas where I had deep knowledge. It was the way I would apologize for taking up space, for having needs, for existing with opinions that might differ from those around me.

The most painful part wasn't the silence itself—it was the gradual disconnection from my own inner knowing. I had become so focused on managing others' reactions that I had stopped paying attention to my own. I was living my life as a series of responses to other people's expectations rather than as an expression of my own truth.

You Are Not Alone in This

If you are anything like me, you are somewhat aware that you have been keeping yourself small and quiet when you have a lot more to say and express. I understand. A lot of us are encouraged by our socialization, factors in our upbringing, or specific conflicts and events as we grow up, to hold ourselves inside and hide ourselves from the world.

Perhaps you were the child who was told to be seen and not heard. Maybe you learned early that your emotions were "too much" or that your questions were inconvenient. You might have grown up in a family where conflict was avoided at all costs, where keeping the peace was everyone's job, where rocking the boat was the worst thing you could do. Or perhaps you had experiences where speaking up led to rejection, criticism, or punishment, teaching you that silence was the safer choice.

For women, especially, these messages are often amplified by cultural expectations. We're praised for being accommodating, for being "easy to work with," for not making waves. We learn that our value lies in our ability to support others, to smooth over conflicts, to make everyone else comfortable—often at the expense of our own comfort and truth.

This was true for my coaching client Amy, who encouraged me to share her story so that others might learn from what she now recognizes as early conditioning—not "mistakes." As a child, Amy was praised for accommodating her "picky" twin sister. She recalls how, when relatives brought them dolls or clothes, her sister would whine or throw a tantrum if she didn't get her preferred color or item. Without being asked, Amy would give in, letting her sister choose first. Her parents applauded this behavior, calling her a "good girl" for being so cooperative. Over time, this praise reinforced a pattern of self-sacrifice and learned compliance.

Fast forward to today: Amy is in her sixties and has only recently realized how deeply this pattern has shaped her life. Prioritizing others' needs became automatic. Her sister grew more entitled, expecting to be accommodated without question, while Amy became the default caregiver in the family. The more Amy stepped up, the more others stepped back. For the past 15 years, she's been solely responsible for transporting elderly relatives to medical appointments, overseeing home health care, and managing their finances as their cognitive decline progressed.

When Amy finally expressed that she couldn't keep doing it all, she was met with exasperation and indifference. Her sister flatly refused to help, and no one else offered support—because everyone had grown accustomed to Amy taking care of everything. Speaking up came late, after years of silence had cemented expectations. Now, with no extended family to share the burden, Amy carries the weight alone and is stretched beyond her limits.

These patterns don't develop in a vacuum. They're survival strategies that once served us, ways of navigating relationships and environments that felt safer when we were smaller, quieter, less visible. But what protected us then may be limiting us now, keeping us from the fullness of who we're meant to be.

And then there's my story! I'll never forget this particular day. I was in the conference room with the other newly hired long-term care surveyors—nursing home inspectors—when the director of the agency called a meeting. It seemed like a routine check-in, just to ask how our training was going. I guess I was naive. At the time, I believed that when someone asked a question, they genuinely wanted an honest answer.

So when it was my turn to speak, I laid it all out. I described the gaps in the training, especially the lack of support from the seasoned nurses who were supposed to be guiding me. Not only were they not training me—they were ignoring me entirely, along with serious issues I had identified in the facilities: concerns about patient choice, inadequate supervision, and other critical problems. As the social worker on the team, I believed it was my responsibility to dig deeper and speak up about what wasn't working.

While shadowing the nurses, they made it clear that there were only certain things they planned to look for and document. But I saw more, and I said so. I gave a detailed account of the obstacles I was facing—not to complain, but because I truly believed the director wanted the truth.

The next thing I knew, I was called into my supervisor's office. She handed me a disciplinary write-up claiming I had made outbursts and disparaging remarks.

I was stunned. I had spoken calmly and truthfully. I wrote a rebuttal and started looking for a way out of the job as quickly as I could. But I needed the income and couldn't risk being fired or leaving with a bad reference. So in the meantime, I tiptoed around on my best—and quietest—behavior, doing everything I could not to draw attention to myself.

That moment marked something deeper than just a misunderstanding—it was the first time I realized that telling the truth could come at a cost. I hadn't raised my voice. I hadn't disrespected anyone. I had simply named what was wrong. And yet, the response was swift and punishing. I wasn't just reprimanded—I was silenced. What I learned that day stayed with me: sometimes, the system doesn't want the truth. It wants silence dressed as professionalism.

Why This Step Changes Everything

Starting with Look Within is vitally important because awareness is the foundation upon which all lasting change is built. Without it, we remain trapped in unconscious patterns, reacting rather than responding, defending rather than expressing, surviving rather than thriving.

When we lack awareness of our silence patterns, we often blame external circumstances. We tell ourselves we don't speak up because our boss is difficult, because our family won't understand, because the timing isn't right, or because the environment feels unsafe. While these factors may be real, they're not the whole story. The deeper truth is that we've internalized beliefs about our voice, our worth, and our right to be heard—beliefs rooted in past experiences, cultural conditioning, fear of rejection, and even self-doubt—that keep us small regardless of the circumstances.

Awareness allows us to see these patterns clearly, to understand the difference between external obstacles and internal barriers. It helps us recognize when we're operating from old programming rather than current reality. Most importantly, it gives us the power to choose differently.

We may fear conflict or worry about damaging relationships. We might believe that our opinions aren't valuable or that speaking up will make us vulnerable or unlovable. Sometimes, we carry unspoken messages from childhood about staying quiet to be "good," "safe," or "likable." These internal barriers often operate beneath our conscious awareness, quietly shaping our behavior more than any external situation.

What Awareness Looks Like in Real Life

In real life, developing awareness looks like catching yourself in the act of self-silencing. It's noticing when you're about to apologize for something that doesn't require an apology. It's recognizing when you're about to agree with something you actually disagree with. It's observing the physical sensations that arise when you consider speaking up—the tightness in your chest, the flutter in your stomach, the way your voice gets smaller.

It's also about recognizing the stories you tell yourself about why you can't speak up. "I don't want to hurt their feelings." "I might be wrong." "It's not that important." "I don't want to seem difficult." These stories often reveal our deepest fears about what will happen if we claim our voice.

Sarah, a client of mine, began to notice that she always prefaced her opinions with phrases like "I might be wrong, but..." or "This probably doesn't matter, but..." She realized she was preemptively diminishing her own voice, giving others permission to dismiss her before she even finished speaking. This awareness was the first step in helping her claim her space in conversations.

Another client, Maria, noticed that she would physically shrink when she disagreed with someone—her shoulders would round, her voice would get quieter, her posture would become smaller. She was literally making herself disappear. Once she became aware of this pattern, she could begin to practice staying physically present even when her instinct was to shrink.

The Science Behind the Silence

Research in neuroscience shows us that our brains are wired to detect threats, and for many of us, speaking up triggers our threat-detection system. When we perceive the risk of rejection, criticism, or conflict, our amygdala—the brain's alarm system—fires up, flooding our system with stress hormones that can literally shut down our ability to think clearly and speak confidently.

This isn't a character flaw or a sign of weakness. It's a normal human response to perceived danger. The problem is that our brains often can't distinguish between actual physical danger and social discomfort. The same system that would protect us from a predator also kicks in when we're about to disagree with our boss or set a boundary with a friend.

Understanding this helps us approach our silence patterns with compassion rather than judgment. We're not broken or cowardly—we're human beings whose nervous systems are trying to keep us safe. But we can learn to expand our window of tolerance, to stay present and connected to our voice even when things feel uncomfortable.

Reclaiming Your Truth Through Awareness

How does awareness foster reclaiming your true self? It starts with the radical act of witnessing yourself without judgment. When you can observe your patterns with curiosity rather than criticism, you create space for change. You begin to see that your silence is not a fixed part of who you are—it's a learned behavior that can be unlearned.

When you Look Within, you reconnect with your inner wisdom. Beneath the layers of conditioning and fear, you may intuitively know or find it easy to discover what's right for you, what you need, what you believe. But this wisdom gets buried under the noise of others' expectations and your own self-doubt. When you turn up the volume on your inner voice, you can begin to hear it again.

This process isn't always comfortable. As you become more aware of how often you silence yourself, you might feel frustrated or disappointed. You might grieve the opportunities you missed, the words you didn't say, the parts of yourself you've kept hidden. This is normal and necessary. Awareness often brings grief before it brings liberation.

The Foundation for All Change

We cannot begin to change or express what we are not aware

of, so it's crucially important that you not try to move into action without doing a comprehensive deep dive into your awareness step. It just won't work.

I've seen too many people try to skip this step, to jump straight into techniques and strategies without first understanding their own patterns. They read about assertiveness skills, practice confident body language, memorize scripts for difficult conversations—but when the moment comes, they still find themselves frozen, still hear their voice getting smaller, still feel that familiar tightness in their chest.

This happens because they're trying to overlay new behaviors on top of old programming without first examining what's underneath. It's like trying to paint over rust without first cleaning the surface—the new paint might look good initially, but it won't last.

The awareness step requires patience and commitment. It asks you to slow down, to pay attention, to sit with uncomfortable truths about how you've been showing up in the world. It requires you to look honestly at the ways you've been complicit in your own silencing, not to blame yourself, but to understand the patterns so you can change them.

Turning Up the Volume

When you turn up the volume on your inner voice, you can finally hear yourself. Until you hear what you have to say—and what you have *not* said, and maybe some of the factors and fears behind keeping yourself small and quiet—you cannot accept the truth of how you show up in the world today.

Think of this process like tuning a radio. When you first turn it on, you might hear static, competing signals, and unclear reception. But as you carefully adjust the dial, focusing on the frequency you want, the signal becomes clearer. Your voice has been there all along, broadcasting on its own frequency, but it's been drowned out by the noise of others' expectations, your own fears, and the habits of silence you've developed over time.

Turning up the volume means learning to distinguish between your voice and the other voices in your head—the inner critic that tells you you're not smart enough, the people-pleaser that insists everyone else's needs come first, the perfectionist that says you must have all the answers before you can speak. These voices are loud and familiar, but they're not your true voice.

Your true voice is the one that knows what you need, that recognizes when something isn't right, that has insights worth sharing. It's the voice that whispers your values, that nudges you toward your dreams, that tells you when a boundary has been crossed. It's been there all along, waiting for you to turn up the volume and listen.

The Mirror of Truth

As you develop awareness, you begin to see yourself more clearly—not the version of yourself you think you should be, not the version others expect you to be, but the version you actually are. This can be both liberating and terrifying. Liberation comes from finally seeing and accepting your authentic self. Terror comes from realizing how much of that self you've been hiding.

But here's the truth: You cannot change what you cannot

accept. And you cannot accept what you cannot see. Awareness is the mirror that reflects back your current reality, not to shame you but to show you where you are so you can decide where you want to go.

This mirror shows you not just your patterns of silence but also your moments of authentic expression. It reveals the times when you did speak up, when you did honor your truth, when you did claim your space. These moments are equally important to notice because they show you that you already have the capacity for authentic expression—you just need to expand it.

The Landscape of Your Silence

Awareness reveals the landscape of your silence—the specific situations, relationships, and contexts where you're most likely to shrink. Maybe you're confident in professional settings but struggle to speak up in your family. Maybe you can advocate for others but not for yourself. Maybe you're fine with small disagreements but shut down when the stakes feel high.

Understanding this landscape helps you see that your silence isn't a blanket pattern—it's more nuanced and context-dependent than you might think. This is actually good news because it means you're not broken or hopeless. You already have some areas of strength to build on.

Lisa, a teacher and mother of three, discovered that she could speak up powerfully for her students and her children, but completely lost her voice when it came to her own needs in her marriage. This awareness helped her understand that she had the skills—she just needed to learn to apply them to *herself*.

The Ripple Effects

As you become more aware of your silence patterns, you'll likely notice how they affect not just you but everyone around you. Your family learns they can make decisions without consulting you. Your colleagues learn they can pile extra work on your plate without pushback. Your friends learn they can dominate conversations without sharing space.

This isn't necessarily malicious—people often don't realize they're overstepping because you haven't shown them your boundaries. But the effects are real. When you consistently silence yourself, you train others to silence you too. When you don't advocate for your needs, others learn it's okay not to consider them.

The flip side is also true: When you begin to speak up, you give others permission to do the same. When you model authentic expression, you create space for others to be authentic too. Your voice doesn't just liberate you—it can liberate others.

Integration and Moving Forward

Awareness is not a one-time achievement but an ongoing practice. As you grow and change, new patterns may emerge. As you enter new situations and relationships, you may discover new ways you silence yourself. This is normal and expected. The goal isn't to achieve perfect awareness but to develop the skill of awareness—the ability to notice, to witness, to see yourself clearly in each moment.

The awareness step has shown you where you are now. You've turned up the volume on your inner voice and begun to hear what it has to say. You've identified the patterns that keep you small and quiet, and you've started to understand the fears and beliefs that drive these patterns. You've seen yourself clearly, perhaps for the first time in a long time.

This awareness is not meant to shame you or make you feel bad about how you've been showing up. It's meant to inform you, to give you the information you need to make different choices. Every moment of awareness is a moment of potential change. Every time you catch yourself in the act of self-silencing, you have the opportunity to choose differently.

The journey from silence to voice begins with this first, essential step: seeing yourself clearly, accepting where you are, and recognizing that change is possible. You have spent years learning to be small and quiet. Now it's time to learn to be loud and proud of who you are.

Ready for the Spotlight

Nice work. It's time to shine a spotlight on what you uncovered in this step, so you understand the meaning and context of this truth. When you can do that, you can accept it as it is without judgment, and that's what is required to have a realistic template for change.

The awareness you've developed isn't just information—it's the foundation for transformation. In the next chapter, we'll take what you've discovered and examine it more closely, understanding not just what your patterns are but why they exist and how they've served you. Only when you understand the full context of your silence can you begin to consciously choose when to speak and when to stay quiet—not from fear, but from wisdom.

You are no longer unconsciously silent. You are aware, awake, and ready to reclaim your voice. The volume is turned up, and you're finally ready to hear what you have to say.

STEP 2: OWN YOUR VOICE

(Shine A Spotlight)

I don't remember exactly when it started—just that by the time I was old enough to tie my own shoes, I was already trying to hold my family together. My parents' marriage was a battlefield, and I became the buffer: the peacemaker, the fixer, the emotional translator.

My mother had a way of filling every room, every conversation, every moment. Her needs were urgent. Her moods, unpredictable. I learned to read her tone before I entered a room, to modulate my voice, to anticipate what would keep the peace. I understood quickly that my own feelings were less important than keeping things calm—that being helpful was the fastest path to safety.

Somewhere along the way, I stopped being a child and became a role: responsible, agreeable, invisible. I didn't choose to disappear; it just seemed like the only way to survive.

In those moments, I learned a lesson that would shape

the next decades of my life: my feelings were secondary to everyone else's needs. My voice was less important than keeping the peace. My presence was valuable only insofar as it served others. I became invisible not because I chose to, but because it felt like the only way to survive.

The years that followed were marked by a persistent sense of disconnection from myself. I moved through life like an actor playing a role—a helpful daughter, the responsible student, the accommodating friend. I became skilled at reading rooms and adjusting myself accordingly, but I lost touch with what I actually wanted, needed, or believed. The darkness and negativity that had permeated my childhood home seemed to follow me everywhere, whispering that I wasn't worth listening to, that my opinions didn't matter, that I should be grateful for whatever scraps of attention or affection came my way.

For years, I carried this story like a weight. I believed that this was simply who I was—someone shaped by loss and negativity, someone destined to fade into the background. I thought that accepting this reality meant resigning myself to it, that making peace with my past meant staying trapped by it. I was wrong.

The breakthrough came not when I tried to change my story, but when I finally learned to accept it fully—all of it, including the parts that felt too painful to acknowledge. I realized that the very experiences that had taught me to become invisible had also given me profound gifts: deep empathy, the ability to hold space for others' pain, and an understanding of human resilience that would serve me throughout my career in social work. The darkness I had tried so hard to escape had actually been preparing me for a life of service, teaching me to see light in even the most difficult circumstances.

Making peace with my story didn't mean excusing the damage or pretending it didn't hurt. It meant recognizing that my invisibility had been a survival strategy—imperfect, but necessary at the time. It meant acknowledging that the little girl who learned to disappear had done the best she could with the tools she had. And it meant understanding that the woman I had become could choose differently, not despite her past but because of the wisdom it had given her.

The Essential Foundation of Acceptance

Acceptance was absolutely essential to being able to change myself. Without it, I would have remained trapped in a cycle of shame and resistance that kept me stuck in old patterns. I spent years trying to bulldoze my way past my history, to overcome my tendencies through sheer force of will. But you cannot build a sustainable new self on a foundation of rejection and self-criticism.

Acceptance doesn't mean approval or resignation. It means acknowledging what is without the filters of what should be or could have been. It means seeing your story clearly—the good, the bad, and the complicated—and recognizing that all of it has contributed to who you are today. It means understanding that your coping mechanisms, even the ones that no longer serve you, were developed for good reasons.

When I finally accepted that my tendency to disappear was a learned response to trauma, I could begin to work with it rather than against it. Instead of berating myself for being "weak" or "invisible," I could appreciate the strength it had taken to survive, and then consciously choose when to step forward and when to step back. Acceptance gave me the freedom to change because I was no longer using all my energy fighting against my own history.

This shift from resistance to acceptance changed everything. Instead of seeing my sensitivity as a flaw, I began to recognize it as a superpower that allowed me to connect deeply with others. Instead of viewing my careful observation of others as people-pleasing, I started to see it as a valuable skill that helped me understand and support people in crisis. Instead of judging my quietness as a weakness, I began to appreciate it as a foundation for thoughtful, intentional speech.

You Are Not Alone in This Struggle

If, like me, you find it really hard to accept the way things happened or the way you responded to them, you're hardly alone. This resistance and shame is, however, frequently why so many people have such a hard time formulating a plan to change things about themselves and having those changes stick, because there's an element that remains untethered from the truth as it is at the beginning.

Most of us have been conditioned to believe that accepting our flaws or difficult experiences means giving up on growth and change. We think that if we stop fighting against our past, we'll somehow become stuck in it. We worry that if we're not constantly criticizing ourselves, we'll become complacent. We fear that acceptance means lowering our standards or excusing harmful behavior.

But this couldn't be further from the truth. Resistance and shame actually keep us trapped in the very patterns we're trying to change. When we're constantly battling against aspects of ourselves, we're using our energy for internal warfare rather than forward movement. When we're ashamed of our history, we're more likely to repeat it because we're not willing to examine it honestly.

Maya, one of my clients, spent years trying to overcome her "people-pleasing" tendencies through willpower alone. She would force herself to say no to requests, then feel guilty and anxious about it. She would practice assertive responses in the mirror, but freeze up when it came time to use them. It wasn't until she accepted that her people-pleasing had developed as a way to feel safe and loved in a chaotic childhood that she could begin to change it. Once she understood and accepted the function it had served, she could make conscious choices about when to accommodate others and when to prioritize her own needs.

The shame we feel about our patterns of silence often runs deeper than we realize. It's not just shame about staying quiet—it's shame about the experiences that taught us to be quiet, shame about our sensitivity, shame about our needs, shame about taking up space. This shame creates an internal environment that's hostile to change. How can you nurture new growth in soil that's been poisoned by self-criticism?

The Deep Work of Full Acceptance

In order to complete the work of acceptance, you have to be fully aware of all the things that factor into your loss of voice, self, and presence. In order to take full responsibility for changing the way this impacts your life, you have to be able to do the deep work of acceptance. You cannot take responsibility and distance yourself from its truth at the same time.

This means accepting not just the obvious factors—the critical parent, the traumatic event, the toxic relationship—but also the subtle influences that shaped your relationship with your voice. It means acknowledging the cultural messages you absorbed about women's roles, the family dynamics that taught you to read the room, and the experiences that convinced you that your needs were secondary to others' comfort.

It also means accepting your own role in maintaining these patterns. This is often the hardest part because it requires acknowledging that you have been complicit in your own silencing. Not because you're weak or broken, but because you made the best choices you could with the information and resources you had at the time.

When I first began this work, I wanted to blame everyone else for my invisibility. My father—for dying too soon. My mother—for her unpredictability and emotional volatility. My family—for always needing me to be the strong one. My colleagues—for overlooking me. My friends—for never asking what I needed.

The truth is, all of these things mattered. They shaped me. But as long as I stayed focused on what others had done or failed to do, I remained stuck. Blame may have felt justified, but it kept me powerless. I couldn't change the past or control other people—but I could take ownership of how I was showing up in my life now. That's where my power was. That's where change could begin.

Taking responsibility doesn't mean taking blame. It means recognizing that you have agency in your own life, that your choices matter, and that you can influence your future even if you couldn't control your past. It means owning both your wounds and your wisdom, your triggers and your strengths, your history and your potential.

The Neuroscience of Acceptance

Research in neuroscience and psychology shows us that acceptance actually creates the optimal conditions for change. When we're in a state of self-criticism and resistance, our brains are flooded with stress hormones that impair our ability to think clearly, learn new patterns, and regulate our emotions. The prefrontal cortex—the part of the brain responsible for executive function and decision-making—goes offline, and we default to automatic, habitual responses.

Acceptance, on the other hand, activates the parasympathetic nervous system, creating a state of calm alertness that's conducive to learning and growth. When we're not using our energy to fight against reality, we can use it to create new possibilities. When we're not defending against our own experience, we can be curious about it and learn from it.

This is why mindfulness-based approaches to change are so effective. They start with acceptance of present-moment experience, creating the neurological conditions necessary for sustainable transformation. Self-compassion research shows that people who treat themselves with kindness and understanding are more likely to make positive changes than those who rely on self-criticism and shame.

Dr. Kristin Neff's research on self-compassion demonstrates that when we respond to our own suffering with the same kindness we'd show a good friend, we're more resilient, more motivated, and more likely to learn from our mistakes. This isn't about lowering standards or making excuses—it's about creating the internal conditions that support growth and change.

The Spotlight That Illuminates Without Judgment

The central principle of the Own Your Voice step is this: You cannot change what you cannot see clearly, and you cannot see clearly what you're afraid to look at. The spotlight of acceptance illuminates your patterns without the harsh glare of judgment, creating the clarity necessary for conscious choice.

Think of this like the difference between examining something under a fluorescent light versus a warm, natural light. The fluorescent light might reveal every flaw and imperfection, but it's harsh and unflattering, making you want to look away. The warm light reveals the same details, but in a way that's easier to tolerate, allowing you to really see what you're working with.

Most of us have been shining the fluorescent light of criticism on ourselves for so long that we've learned to look away from what we don't want to see. We know we have patterns of silence, but we don't want to examine them too closely because we're afraid of what we might find. We might discover that we're more afraid than we want to admit, more wounded than we'd like to acknowledge, more complicit in our own suffering than we're comfortable facing.

But this avoidance keeps us stuck. We can't change patterns we refuse to see clearly. We can't heal wounds we won't acknowledge. We can't take responsibility for choices we won't examine honestly.

The spotlight of acceptance allows us to see our patterns clearly without being overwhelmed by shame or self-criticism. It illuminates the full picture—not just our struggles but also our strengths, not just our wounds but also our wisdom, not just our automatic responses but also our capacity for conscious choice.

How Acceptance Supports Finding Your Self

When you can accept your story fully—including the parts that feel uncomfortable or painful—you reclaim all the parts of yourself that you've been trying to hide or fix. You discover that your sensitivity isn't a flaw but a gift. Your careful observation of others isn't just people-pleasing but also emotional intelligence. Your tendency to step back isn't only avoidance but also thoughtful reflection.

This integration of rejected parts of yourself creates a more complete, authentic sense of self. Instead of trying to be someone you're not, you can become more fully who you are. Instead of spending energy maintaining a false persona, you can use that energy to express your truth. Instead of feeling fragmented and conflicted, you can feel whole and aligned.

Marcus, a client who struggled with speaking up in his corporate job, discovered that his quiet nature wasn't a professional liability but an asset. His colleagues valued his thoughtful input when he did speak because they knew he'd carefully considered his words. His tendency to listen more than he talked made him an excellent manager because his team felt heard and understood. Once he accepted these aspects of himself, he could use them strategically rather than apologizing for them.

Finding yourself through acceptance also means recognizing that you don't have to be perfect to be valuable. You don't have to have all the answers to contribute to conversations. You don't have to be the loudest person in the room to be heard. You don't have to eliminate all your fears to act courageously. You can be flawed and worthy, scared and brave, quiet and powerful all at the same time.

Creating Your Life from an Authentic Foundation

When you're operating from a place of self-acceptance, you make choices based on your true values and desires rather than on fear, shame, or the need to prove your worth. You're no longer trying to compensate for perceived deficiencies or hide parts of yourself you find unacceptable. You're creating from a place of wholeness rather than from a place of lack.

This doesn't mean you become selfish or stop caring about others. It means you include yourself in your circle of care. It means you recognize that your needs matter, that your voice has value, that your presence is a gift rather than a burden. It means you understand that you can serve others more effectively when you're not constantly depleting yourself.

Creating your life from this foundation of acceptance looks different for everyone. For some, it means finally pursuing that career change they've been putting off. For others, it means setting boundaries in relationships that have been one-sided.

For some, it means speaking up in meetings or social situations. For others, it means allowing themselves to be seen and known more fully.

The key is that these choices come from authenticity rather than from trying to prove something or overcome something.

They come from a place of self-respect rather than self-improvement. They come from knowing who you are and what you need rather than from trying to be someone you're not.

The Cost of Avoiding the Spotlight

What happens if you do not Shine A Spotlight on your patterns with acceptance? Your frustrated feelings continue to infect what you try to change. You remain trapped in cycles of shame and resistance that undermine your efforts at growth. You try to build new behaviors on a foundation of self-rejection, which makes them unstable and unsustainable.

Without acceptance, your attempts at change often become another form of self-criticism. You try to force yourself to speak up, then berate yourself when you don't. You practice assertive responses, then feel like a failure when you revert to old patterns. You set goals for change, then abandon them when they feel too difficult or when you don't see immediate results.

This creates a vicious cycle where your failure to change becomes more evidence of your inadequacy, which reinforces the shame and self-criticism that made change difficult in the first place. You become frustrated with yourself, which makes you more likely to retreat into familiar patterns of silence and invisibility.

I see this with clients who come to me having tried multiple approaches to building confidence and finding their voice. They've read the books, attended the workshops, and practiced the techniques, but they're still struggling. When we dig deeper, we often discover that they've been trying to change themselves without ever accepting themselves. They've been trying to overcome their sensitivity, fix their people-pleasing, eliminate their anxiety—but you can't successfully change something you're at war with.

The frustrated feelings that come from failed attempts at change don't just disappear. They accumulate and create an internal environment that's hostile to growth. Every setback becomes evidence that you're hopeless, every struggle becomes proof that you're broken, every moment of silence becomes confirmation that you'll never find your voice.

The Transformative Power of Radical Acceptance

When Rebecca first came to work with me, she was angry—at herself, at her family, at the circumstances that had shaped her. She had grown up in a household where her father's explosive temper dominated every interaction, where speaking up meant risking his rage, where invisibility felt like survival. As an adult, she found herself unable to advocate for herself at work, unable to set boundaries with her own family, and unable to speak up even when her silence was costing her opportunities and relationships.

She had tried everything she could think of to change these patterns. She had practiced assertive responses, role-played difficult conversations, and even taken a public speaking class. But nothing stuck. In our sessions, she would alternate between berating herself for being "weak" and raging against the circumstances that had made her this way.

The breakthrough came when she finally allowed herself to feel compassion for the little girl who had learned to disappear. Instead of seeing her silence as a character flaw, she began to understand it as a brilliant survival strategy. Instead of judging her sensitivity as a weakness, she recognized it as a superpower that had helped her navigate dangerous emotional terrain.

This shift in perspective changed everything. She could finally see that her careful attention to others' emotions wasn't just people-pleasing—it was emotional intelligence. Her tendency to think before speaking wasn't just fear—it was thoughtfulness. Her ability to remain calm in tense situations wasn't just freezing—it was grace under pressure.

Once she accepted these aspects of herself, she could use them strategically. She could choose when to speak and when to listen, when to step forward and when to step back. She could honor her sensitivity while also honoring her need to be heard. She could be both thoughtful and assertive, both caring and boundaried.

The Ripple Effects of Self-Acceptance

When you accept yourself fully, you give others permission to do the same. Your willingness to be imperfect and human creates space for others to be imperfect and human. Your modeling of self-compassion teaches others that they, too, can be gentle with themselves. Your integration of all parts of yourself—the strong and the vulnerable, the confident and the uncertain—shows others that wholeness is possible.

This doesn't mean you become complacent or stop growing. It means you grow from a place of love rather than from a place of lack. You change because you want to expand and evolve, not because you're trying to fix something that's broken. You take risks because you're curious about your potential, not because you're trying to prove your worth.

The people in your life may notice these changes before you do. They might comment that you seem more relaxed, more present, more authentic. They might find themselves being more honest with you because you're being more honest with yourself. They might feel safer to be vulnerable because you're no longer hiding your own vulnerability.

Developing acceptance is not a one-time event but an ongoing practice. Here are some ways to deepen your relationship with yourself:

<u>Practice Self-Compassion</u>: When you notice yourself being self-critical, pause and ask: "What would I say to a good friend in this situation?" Speak to yourself with the same kindness you'd offer someone you care about.

<u>Acknowledge Your Survival Strategies</u>: Instead of judging your patterns of silence, recognize them as strategies that once helped you survive. Thank them for their service, even as you choose to modify them.

<u>Explore Your Story Without Judgment</u>: Write about your experiences without trying to make them into a neat narrative. Let the contradictions and complexities exist without trying to resolve them.

<u>Notice Your Wholeness</u>: Pay attention to all aspects of yourself—your strengths and struggles, your wisdom and wounds, your confidence and uncertainty. Practice seeing yourself as a complete person rather than a collection of problems to be solved.

<u>Honor Your Sensitivity</u>: If you're highly sensitive, recognize this as a gift rather than a curse. Your ability to pick up on subtle cues and feel things deeply is a superpower, even if it sometimes feels overwhelming.

The Light of Understanding

Shining a spotlight on your patterns through acceptance illuminates not just what needs to change, but also what needs to be honored and preserved. It reveals the full picture of who you are—not just the parts you want to improve, but also the parts that are already working beautifully.

This comprehensive view of yourself creates a solid foundation for change. You're no longer trying to eliminate parts of yourself or become someone entirely different. You're working with your authentic self, using your existing strengths and addressing your real challenges. You're growing from the inside out rather than trying to paste new behaviors onto an unchanged core.

The spotlight also reveals your resilience. When you look honestly at what you've survived, what you've learned, and how you've adapted, you can't help but be impressed by your own strength. You begin to see that if you could survive and thrive despite difficult circumstances, you can certainly learn to speak up and claim your space in the world.

Key Points of Shining the Spotlight

The Shine A Spotlight step is about making peace with your story so you can write a new chapter. It requires:

Full Acceptance: Embracing all aspects of your experience without judgment or the need to change them immediately.

Compassionate Understanding: Recognizing that your patterns of silence developed for good reasons and served important functions.

Integration: Seeing yourself as a whole person rather than a collection of problems to be solved.

Responsibility Without Blame: Taking ownership of your role in maintaining these patterns without shaming yourself for having them.

Foundation for Change: Creating the internal conditions—self-compassion, clarity, and wholeness—that support sustainable transformation.

When you can see your patterns clearly without being overwhelmed by shame or self-criticism, you create the possibility for conscious choice. When you can accept your story fully, you reclaim the parts of yourself that you've been trying to hide or fix. When you can honor your sensitivity and thoughtfulness while also claiming your voice, you become unstoppable.

Ready to Take the Wheel

You've done the hard work of turning up the volume on your inner voice and shining a spotlight on your patterns with acceptance and compassion. You've made peace with your story and reclaimed all the parts of yourself that you've been trying to hide or fix. You've created a foundation of self-acceptance that can support lasting change.

Now it's time for the next step: Take the Wheel. This is where you move from understanding to action, from acceptance to intentional change. You've learned to see yourself clearly and accept what you find. Now you get to decide what to do with that information.

Taking the wheel means recognizing that you have agency in

your own life. You may not be able to control what happens to you, but you can influence how you respond. You may not be able to change your history, but you can change your future. You may not be able to eliminate all your fears, but you can learn to act courageously despite them.

The wheel is in your hands. You know who you are, you understand why you've been silent, and you've made peace with your story. Now it's time to decide where you want to go and start steering your life in that direction. The journey continues, but you're no longer a passenger—you're the driver.

Are you ready to take the wheel and start creating the life you've always wanted? The spotlight has shown you the truth of who you are. Now it's time to use that truth to build something beautiful.

STEP 3: UNDERSTAND YOUR POWER

(Take the Wheel)

I was sitting in my car in the parking lot of the psychiatric hospital where I'd worked for years, staring at the wall after yet another difficult conversation with my supervisor. My hands were shaking—not from fear, but from the familiar cocktail of frustration and helplessness that had become my constant companion. I'd just been told, once again, that my concerns about organizational practices were "duly noted" and that I should "focus on my own responsibilities."

But I had changed. I finally understood that if anything was going to be different, it had to start with me taking complete ownership of my response to the situation.

"If it is to be, it is up to me." Those words echoed in my mind as I made a decision that would reshape not just my career, but my entire relationship with my own voice and agency.

For months, I'd been watching practices that didn't align with what I knew was best for our patients. I'd been bringing up concerns in staff meetings, only to be subtly dismissed or redirected. I'd been having conversations with colleagues who agreed with me behind closed doors but stayed silent in meetings. And I'd been going home each night feeling like I was failing the very people I'd entered this profession to help.

That day in the parking lot, something shifted. As I sat there replaying the conversation, I realized I'd been waiting—waiting for someone else to speak up, waiting for the system to change itself, waiting for permission to use my voice in a way that mattered. I'd been treating myself like a passenger in my own professional life, hoping someone else would take the wheel and drive us in the right direction.

However, letting that frustration build had taken me to the other side. Using my voice reactively and provocatively, and without sensitivity to the rules and protocols of the situation I was working within. I had taken myself out of silence and passivity, but I was not yet using my voice with as much awareness and acceptance as I would later be able to do with the work of steps 1 and 2 integrated properly and well.

The Passenger Seat Pattern

Looking back, I can see clearly how I'd been operating from what I now call the "passenger seat" of my own life. I was present, I was engaged, I was even offering suggestions about the route—but I wasn't taking responsibility for the destination. I was letting other people's comfort levels, institutional inertia, and my own fear of conflict determine how I showed up in situations that mattered to me.

This wasn't malicious or intentional. I genuinely believed I was being professional, collaborative, and respectful. I thought

I was following the right protocols by bringing concerns to the appropriate channels and waiting for others to act. I told myself I was being "strategic" by not pushing too hard, not making waves, not risking my position or relationships.

But underneath all these reasonable explanations was a deeper truth: I was avoiding the weight of full responsibility. *Taking the wheel meant accepting that the outcomes in my life—both the ones I wanted and the ones I didn't—were largely within my control. It meant acknowledging that my voice had power, and that with that power came the responsibility to use it wisely and courageously.*

Before that parking lot moment, I'd been operating under the unconscious belief that someone else should go first. Someone else should take the risk. Someone else should handle the difficult conversations. I was willing to support change, but I wasn't willing to be the one who initiated it.

I wanted transformation, but I wanted it to happen *around* me, not *through* me. Then, when I got hot under the collar enough that I *had* to say something or I was going to lose it, it backfired spectacularly.

Where had I missed the connection between thought and execution? Was it just not an environment that would allow the truth? Or was there a step missing that I had yet to discover?

This pattern showed up everywhere once I started paying attention. In family dynamics, I'd hint at problems but wait for others to address them directly. In friendships, I'd silently tolerate behaviors that bothered me rather than risk an uncomfortable conversation. Even in my personal goals, I'd make plans and wait for the "right time" or the "right circumstances" rather than creating the conditions for change myself.

The cost of this passenger seat approach was enormous, though I didn't fully realize it at the time. Every time I deferred my agency to others, I was essentially telling myself that my voice didn't matter enough to risk discomfort. Every time I waited for someone else to speak up, I was reinforcing the belief that change was something that happened to me, not something I could create.

You Are Not Alone in This

If you recognize yourself in this pattern, please know that you're not alone—and there's nothing wrong with you. The passenger seat approach is incredibly common, and it often develops for very good reasons. Many of us learned early in our lives that speaking up could be dangerous, that challenging authority led to negative consequences, or that our role was to support others rather than lead.

Maybe you grew up in a family where questioning decisions was seen as disrespectful. Maybe you learned in school that the squeaky wheel gets replaced, not oiled. Maybe you've had professional experiences where speaking up led to retaliation, or personal experiences where asserting yourself damaged relationships you valued. These experiences create neural pathways that make the passenger seat feel like the safest place to be.

Our culture also reinforces this pattern in countless subtle ways. We praise people for being "team players" and "going with the flow." We celebrate leaders but often criticize those who challenge existing systems. We reward compliance and punish disruption, even when that disruption is necessary for growth or justice.

For many people, especially women, there are additional layers of conditioning that make taking the wheel feel foreign or even selfish. We may have been taught that our primary role is to support others, to maintain harmony, to put everyone else's needs before our own. The idea of taking full responsibility for our own voice and agency can feel like a violation of these deeply ingrained messages.

If you're reading this and thinking, "But I do speak up sometimes," that's valid too. *Taking the wheel isn't about being loud or confrontational all the time. It's about recognizing when you're deferring your power and making a conscious choice to reclaim it. It's about moving from reactive to proactive, from hoping for change to creating it.*

The compassion I want to offer you is this: Wherever you are in this journey is exactly where you need to be right now. The awareness that you might be operating from the passenger seat is the first step toward taking the wheel. You don't have to transform overnight, and you don't have to do it perfectly. You just have to be willing to start.

Why the Wheel Comes First

Understanding why taking the wheel must come before speaking up loudly is crucial to making lasting change. I've seen too many people try to skip this step, jumping straight to assertiveness techniques or communication strategies, only to find themselves back in old patterns when the pressure mounts.

Here's why the sequence matters: When you try to use your

voice without first taking full responsibility for your own agency, you're essentially trying to drive while someone else controls the steering wheel. You might make some noise, you might even move in the right direction for a while, but when you hit a bump in the road or encounter resistance, you'll instinctively hand the wheel back to whoever feels more comfortable holding it.

Taking the wheel means accepting that your voice, your boundaries, your values, and your responses are entirely within your control. It means recognizing that while you can't control other people's reactions, you can control your own actions. It means understanding that you have the power to choose how you show up in any situation, regardless of what others are doing.

Without this foundation of personal responsibility, speaking up becomes a strategy rather than an expression of your authentic power. And strategies can be abandoned when they don't work immediately or when they create discomfort. But when speaking up comes from a place of genuine ownership of your voice, it becomes non-negotiable. It becomes who you are, not just what you do.

Think about it this way: If you're still looking to others for permission to use your voice, what happens when that permission isn't granted? If you're still waiting for the "right" conditions to speak up, what happens when those conditions never come? If you're still hoping that someone else will create the change you want to see, what happens when they don't?

Taking the wheel means recognizing that you already have everything you need to begin. You don't need permission, perfect conditions, or someone else's approval. You need the willingness to accept full responsibility for your own voice and to use it in service of what matters to you.

What It Looks Like When You Don't Take the Wheel

I've witnessed countless examples of what happens when people try to speak up without first taking the wheel, both in my professional work and in my own life. The patterns are remarkably consistent, and they're always heartbreaking because they involve people who genuinely want to create change but end up undermining themselves.

Brianna was a colleague who frequently complained about workplace policies she disagreed with. She'd bring up concerns in meetings, write emails to supervisors, and rally support from other staff members. But when push came to shove, she'd always defer to authority. When a supervisor would push back on her suggestions, she'd quickly back down, saying things like, "Well, you know better than I do," or, "I guess there are things I don't understand about the bigger picture."

Brianna wasn't taking the wheel because she was still operating from the belief that someone else's opinion mattered more than her own. She wanted change, but she wasn't willing to stand behind her convictions when they were challenged. As a result, her voice became background noise rather than a catalyst for transformation.

Then there was Michael, a childhood friend of mine who was struggling in his marriage. He'd grown increasingly frustrated with his wife's spending habits and their lack of communication about finances. He'd tried bringing up his concerns multiple times, but every conversation he had with her ended with him apologizing and agreeing to let her handle the money decisions. He was angry and resentful, but when I asked him what he was going to do differently, he'd say, "I can't control her spending, so I guess I just have to accept it."

Michael wasn't taking the wheel because he was confusing acceptance with resignation. He thought that because he couldn't control his wife's behavior, he had no power in the situation. But he was missing the crucial point: he could control his own responses, his own boundaries, and his own participation in patterns that weren't working for him.

I see this pattern repeatedly in my mediation work as well. People come to the table wanting resolution, but they're still operating from the passenger seat. They want the other party to change, they want the mediator to fix the problem, they want the process to transform their situation—but they're not willing to take full responsibility for their own part in creating a solution.

When you don't take the wheel, you end up in what I call the "complaint loop"—endlessly describing problems without taking action to solve them. You become someone who talks about change rather than someone who creates it. You develop a reputation as someone who has opinions but not convictions, someone who identifies problems but doesn't drive solutions.

Perhaps most damaging, when you don't take the wheel, you reinforce your own sense of powerlessness. Every time you defer your agency, you're telling yourself that you don't have what it takes to create the change you want. Every time you wait for someone else to act, you're confirming the belief that your voice doesn't matter enough to risk discomfort.

The Foundation of Agency

Taking the wheel is fundamentally about reclaiming your personal agency—your ability to act independently and make free choices about your life. Agency isn't just about having options; it's about recognizing that you have the power to exercise those options and accepting full responsibility for the consequences of your choices.

Research in psychology has consistently shown that people with a strong sense of agency are more resilient, more satisfied with their lives, and more effective at creating positive change. They're also more likely to speak up when something matters to them because they understand that their voice is an expression of their power, not a request for someone else's permission.

Agency begins with awareness—recognizing the difference between what you can control and what you can't. You can't control other people's reactions, but you can control your own actions. You can't control outcomes, but you can control your effort and approach. You can't control the past, but you can control how you respond to it in the present.

This awareness creates what psychologists call an "internal locus of control"—the belief that you have the power to influence your own life circumstances. People with an internal locus of control are more likely to take initiative, more likely to persist through challenges, and more likely to recover from setbacks because they see themselves as active participants in their own lives rather than passive recipients of whatever happens to them.

Building agency also requires developing what I call "response-ability"—the ability to choose your response in any situation.

This isn't about controlling your emotions or never feeling overwhelmed. It's about recognizing that even in the most challenging circumstances, you have choices about how you respond. You can choose to speak up or stay silent. You can choose to set boundaries or let them be crossed. You can choose to take action or wait for someone else to act.

The more you practice response-ability, the more natural it becomes. You start to see opportunities for choice where you once saw only limitations. You begin to recognize your own power where you once felt powerless. You develop confidence in your ability to handle whatever comes your way because you know you can choose how to respond.

Agency also involves accepting that with power comes responsibility. When you take the wheel, you're accepting that the direction of your life is largely up to you. This can feel scary at first, especially if you've been comfortable in the passenger seat. But it's also profoundly liberating because it means you're no longer dependent on others for your sense of purpose, direction, or fulfillment.

The Language of Taking the Wheel

One of the most powerful ways to take the wheel is to change the language you use to describe your situation and your choices. Language shapes thought, and thought shapes action. When you start speaking about your life from a place of agency rather than victimhood, you begin to see possibilities where you once saw only problems.

Instead of saying, "I have to," try saying, "I choose to." This simple shift reminds you that most of what you do is actually a choice, even when it doesn't feel like one. You choose to stay in a job that frustrates you because you value financial security. You choose to maintain a relationship that's challenging because you value the connection. You choose to avoid difficult conversations because you value peace over conflict.

Recognizing these as choices doesn't mean they're easy choices or that you should necessarily make different ones. It means acknowledging that you have agency in your life and that you're making decisions based on your values and priorities.

Instead of saying, "They won't let me," try saying, "I haven't yet found a way to." This shift moves you from a position of powerlessness to a position of possibility. It acknowledges that there may be obstacles or challenges, but it also affirms your ability to work with or around them.

Instead of saying, "I can't," try saying, "I don't know how yet." This language keeps you open to learning and growing rather than closing off possibilities. It acknowledges limitations while maintaining hope for change.

Instead of saying, "That's just how it is," try saying, "That's how it's been so far." This shift acknowledges reality while keeping the door open for transformation. It recognizes patterns without accepting them as permanent.

The language of taking the wheel also includes owning your wants and needs without apology. Instead of saying, "I probably shouldn't ask for this, but…" try saying, "I'd like to request…" Instead of saying, "I know this is probably impossible, but…" try saying, "I'm hoping we can find a way to…"

This isn't about being demanding or unreasonable. It's about presenting your needs as legitimate and worth considering. It's about speaking from a place of self-respect rather than self-doubt.

How Taking the Wheel Supports Finding Your Voice

When you take the wheel in your life, you create the conditions necessary for your authentic voice to emerge. Your voice isn't just about the words you speak; it's about the full expression of who you are and what you stand for. But your voice can't fully develop if you're still operating from the passenger seat.

Taking the wheel supports finding your voice by building self-trust. Every time you make a choice from a place of agency rather than default, you demonstrate to yourself that you can be trusted with your own life. Every time you take responsibility for your responses rather than blaming circumstances, you build confidence in your ability to handle whatever comes your way.

This self-trust is essential for voice development because speaking up requires believing that what you have to say matters. If you don't trust yourself to make good decisions, why would you trust yourself to speak up at important moments? If you don't believe in your own agency, why would you believe in the power of your voice?

Taking the wheel also supports finding your voice by clarifying your values and priorities. When you're operating from the passenger seat, you're often responding to whatever seems most urgent or whatever makes others most comfortable. But when you take the wheel, you have to decide where you want to go, which means getting clear about what matters most to you.

This clarity becomes the foundation for your voice. You can't speak authentically about what you don't know you care about. You can't advocate effectively for what you haven't clarified as important. Taking the wheel forces you to examine your values and make conscious choices about how to express them.

Additionally, taking the wheel supports finding your voice by building tolerance for discomfort. When you're in the passenger seat, you're often focused on avoiding conflict, maintaining harmony, and keeping everyone comfortable. But when you take the wheel, you accept that discomfort is part of growth and that meaningful change often requires navigating difficult conversations.

This tolerance for discomfort is crucial for voice development because speaking up almost always involves some level of risk. You might be misunderstood, criticized, or rejected. You might create conflict or disappointment. Taking the wheel means accepting these possibilities and choosing to speak anyway because you understand that your voice matters more than your comfort.

Why the Wheel Comes Before Living Loud

The progression from taking the wheel to living loud isn't arbitrary—it's based on the psychological and practical realities of sustainable change. Living loud means expressing yourself fully, standing up for what you believe in, and refusing to shrink to make others comfortable. But if you try to live loud without first taking the wheel, you'll likely find yourself either burning out or backing down when the pressure mounts.

Living loud requires enormous energy and resilience because it means consistently choosing authenticity over approval, truth over comfort, and growth over safety. This kind of sustained expression is only possible when it comes from a deep sense of personal responsibility and agency. When you take the wheel first, living loud becomes a natural expression of who you are rather than a performance you're putting on.

Think about the people you know who live loud in a way that feels authentic and sustainable. They're not performing loudness—they're expressing their genuine selves. They're not trying to prove anything to anyone—they're simply refusing to hide who they are. This kind of authentic expression is only possible when it comes from a place of deep personal ownership.

When you try to live loud without taking the wheel, you're essentially trying to use someone else's voice. You might copy techniques you've seen others use, or strategies you've read about, but they won't feel natural because they're not coming from your own center of agency. They'll feel forced, and they'll be exhausting to maintain.

Taking the wheel also prepares you for the inevitable challenges that come with living loud. When you express yourself authentically, you will face resistance. People who were comfortable with your previous patterns will push back against your new ones. Systems that benefited from your silence will work to maintain the status quo. Taking the wheel means accepting responsibility for navigating these challenges rather than expecting others to make the path easy for you.

Finally, taking the wheel ensures that your loud living serves your authentic values rather than just your ego. When you haven't taken the wheel, living loud can become about proving yourself, getting attention, or compensating for feelings of powerlessness. But when you take the wheel first, living loud becomes about expressing your truth, serving your values, and contributing to the changes you want to see in the world.

The Key Elements of Taking the Wheel

Taking the wheel isn't a one-time event—it's an ongoing practice that requires attention, intention, and commitment. Here are the key elements that make this practice sustainable and effective:

Radical Responsibility: This means accepting complete ownership of your responses, choices, and outcomes. It doesn't mean blaming yourself for everything that happens, but it does mean recognizing that you always have choices about how to respond to what happens. Radical responsibility is liberating because it puts you in the driver's seat of your own life.

Values Clarification: You can't drive purposefully if you don't know where you're going. Taking the wheel requires getting clear about what matters most to you and making decisions based on those values rather than on what's easiest or most comfortable. This clarity becomes your internal compass for decision-making.

Boundary Setting: Taking the wheel means deciding what you will and won't accept in your life and communicating those boundaries clearly. This isn't about controlling others—it's about controlling your own participation in patterns that don't serve you.

Proactive Decision-Making: Instead of waiting for circumstances to force your hand, taking the wheel means making conscious choices about how you want to show up in your life. This requires moving from reactive to proactive, from responsive to intentional.

Self-Trust Building: Every time you honor your own values, keep your own commitments, and follow through on your own decisions, you build trust in your own judgment. This self-trust is essential for taking the wheel because it gives you confidence in your ability to navigate whatever comes your way.

Discomfort Tolerance: Taking the wheel means accepting that growth and change often involve discomfort. Instead of avoiding difficult conversations or challenging situations, you learn to move through them with grace and purpose.

Your Invitation to Take the Wheel

As we close this chapter, I want to offer you an invitation rather than an instruction. Taking the wheel is a choice that only you can make, and it's a choice that you'll need to make repeatedly as you grow and change.

The invitation is this: start paying attention to the moments when you're operating from the passenger seat. Notice when you're waiting for someone else to take action, when you're hoping for circumstances to change without your input, when you're complaining about problems without taking responsibility for solutions.

In those moments, ask yourself: "What would it look like for me to take the wheel here?" You don't have to act on the answer immediately. You don't have to transform overnight. You just have to begin to see the possibilities that exist when you operate from a place of agency rather than passivity.

Remember that taking the wheel isn't about being perfect or having all the answers. It's about being willing to accept responsibility for your own life and to use your voice in service of what matters to you. It's about recognizing that you already have everything you need to begin—you just need the courage to start driving.

In our next chapter, we'll explore how taking the wheel translates into specific strategies for speaking up in real-time situations. We'll look at practical techniques for using your voice effectively, even when you're feeling nervous or uncertain. But first, you need to accept that the wheel is already in your hands—you just need to decide to use it.

The road ahead may be uncertain, but your ability to navigate it isn't. You have the power to choose your direction, to adjust your course when needed, and to keep moving forward even when the path is unclear. The question isn't whether you're capable of taking the wheel—it's whether you're willing to stop waiting for someone else to do it for you.

Your voice is waiting. Your authentic self is waiting. Your most empowered life is waiting. All that's required is for you to take the wheel and begin driving toward it.

STEP 4: DECIDE TO ACT

(From Silence to Inspired Action)

The first time I truly understood the difference between forced action and inspired action was during my tenure working in the prison system. I'd been facilitating therapy groups for inmates with serious mental illness for a number of days, following the prescribed protocols, checking all the boxes, and delivering the approved curriculum. I was doing everything right according to the manual, but something felt hollow. My actions were technically correct, but they lacked the authenticity that creates a real connection and change.

Then one afternoon, during a particularly difficult group session, I found myself abandoning the lesson plan entirely. One of the participants, Marcus, had been triggered by something another group member said, and instead of redirecting him back to the scheduled activity, I felt an inner pull to simply listen. Not the clinical listening I'd been trained to do, but the deep, compassionate listening that comes from recognizing shared humanity. In that moment, my response wasn't driven by what I thought I should do—it flowed naturally from who I was becoming as both a therapist and a human being.

The conversation that followed was transformative, not just for Marcus, but for the entire group. For the first time in a number of days, I felt the electricity of authentic connection, the power of showing up fully present rather than simply following a script. That session taught me something crucial: when action springs from inner alignment rather than external pressure, it carries a different quality of power. It doesn't drain you—it energizes you. It doesn't feel like work—it feels like expression.

This distinction between forced action and inspired action is the level of emotional work that's gone into understanding who you are and what you need, what parts of your situation you control (and not), and how you need to take the lead to let others know where you are coming from. It's the difference between speaking up because you think you should and speaking up because you must. It's the difference between following someone else's script for assertiveness and expressing your own authentic truth. There are no shortcuts.

The Natural Flow of Authentic Action

After years of working with people who struggle to speak up, I've observed a consistent pattern: Those who maintain their voice over time are those whose actions feel natural and inspired rather than forced. They're not following a script or trying to become someone they're not—they're expressing who they already are, but with greater clarity and courage.

This natural flow happens when action emerges from the work you've already done on the inside. When you've identified your authentic self, owned your voice, and taken the wheel of your life, speaking up stops being something you have to force yourself to do. It becomes something you can't help but do because staying silent would require more energy than speaking your truth.

Think about the difference between trying to push water uphill and allowing it to flow downhill. Forced action is like pushing water uphill—it requires constant effort, creates resistance, and exhausts you quickly. Inspired action is like water flowing downhill—it moves naturally, gains momentum, and carries you forward with ease.

This doesn't mean inspired action is always easy or comfortable. Water flowing downhill still encounters rocks and obstacles. But it doesn't stop flowing because of them—it finds a way around, over, or through. Similarly, when your actions come from authentic inner alignment, you don't abandon them at the first sign of resistance. You find creative ways to maintain your truth while navigating the challenges.

The key is understanding that willpower alone is not sustainable. You can force yourself to speak up for a while, but if that action isn't rooted in genuine self-knowledge and authentic commitment, you'll eventually exhaust yourself and retreat back to silence. Inspired action, on the other hand, is renewable because it comes from a source that regenerates itself—your authentic self.

I've seen this play out repeatedly in mediation work. The agreements that last are the ones where both parties arrive at solutions that feel natural and aligned with their values. The agreements that fall apart are the ones where people force themselves to accept terms that don't truly resonate with them.

The same principle applies to finding your voice—sustainable change happens when action flows from authenticity rather than obligation.

You're Not Alone in This Struggle

If you've been trying to speak up through sheer willpower and finding yourself exhausted or inconsistent, please know that you're not alone. I've been exactly where you are, and I've worked with countless individuals who've experienced the same frustration. The cultural message that we should be able to change our behavior through determination alone has left many people feeling like failures when their forced efforts don't sustain.

I remember my early attempts at being more assertive in professional settings. I would psych myself up before meetings, rehearse what I was going to say, and force myself to speak up even when it felt unnatural. Sometimes it worked in the moment, but I'd leave those interactions feeling drained and somehow inauthentic. I was performing assertiveness rather than expressing it, and the performance was exhausting.

The compassion I want to offer you is this: If you've been trying to skip straight to action without first doing the inner work of finding your authentic self, owning your voice, and taking the wheel of your life, you're not weak or lacking in willpower. You're simply trying to build a house without first laying the foundation. The house might stand for a while, but it won't withstand the storms that inevitably come.

Taking action without the first three steps can only lead to temporary satisfaction because it's not rooted in who you truly are. It's borrowed behavior, and borrowed behavior always feels foreign and requires constant maintenance. You might successfully speak up in a few situations, but you'll find yourself reverting to old patterns when the pressure increases or when you encounter unexpected resistance.

This isn't a character flaw—it's a natural consequence of trying to change from the outside in rather than from the inside out. Real, lasting change in how you use your voice must begin with understanding who you are, what you stand for, and why your voice matters. Without that foundation, even the most sophisticated communication techniques will feel hollow and unsustainable.

The good news is that you don't have to stay stuck in this cycle. Once you understand the difference between forced action and inspired action, you can begin to shift your approach. Instead of trying to become someone you're not, you can focus on becoming more fully who you already are.

When Action Misses the Mark

Let me tell you about Jennifer, a client who came to me after what she called her "failed assertiveness experiment." Jennifer had been struggling with her mother-in-law's constant criticism and unsolicited advice about how she was raising her children. After reading several books on assertiveness and attending a workshop on communication skills, she decided to take action.

The next time her mother-in-law made a critical comment about her parenting, Jennifer used all the techniques she'd learned. She used "I" statements, she set clear boundaries, and she spoke calmly and firmly. Technically, she did everything right. But something went wrong. Instead of feeling empowered, she felt exhausted. Instead of improving the relationship, she created more tension. Instead of finding her voice, she felt like she was wearing a costume that didn't fit.

The problem wasn't with Jennifer's technique—it was with her timing. She had jumped straight to action without first understanding why her mother-in-law's comments affected her so deeply, what she really wanted from the relationship, or how to respond from a place of authentic strength rather than reactive frustration.

When we worked together, Jennifer discovered that her mother-in-law's criticism triggered old childhood wounds about not being good enough. She realized that her silence hadn't been about maintaining peace—it had been about avoiding the vulnerability of standing up for herself. Most importantly, she understood that her desire to speak up wasn't really about changing her mother-in-law's behavior—it was about honoring her own worth as a parent and a person.

Once Jennifer did this inner work, her external actions changed dramatically. She didn't need to use formal assertiveness techniques because her responses came naturally from a place of self-respect and clarity. She could engage with her mother-in-law without being triggered because she understood her own patterns and motivations. She could set boundaries without aggression because she wasn't fighting against her own insecurities.

The conversation that followed was completely different from her previous attempts. It was authentic, respectful, and ultimately more effective because it came from who Jennifer really was rather than who she thought she should be.

This is what I see repeatedly: when people try to take action without first doing the inner work, they often succeed in the short term but fail in the long term. They might speak up once or twice, but they can't sustain it because it doesn't feel natural. They might set boundaries, but they can't maintain them because they're not rooted in genuine self-respect. They might have difficult conversations, but they can't navigate the ongoing relationship challenges because they haven't addressed the underlying patterns that created the problems in the first place.

The Foundation of Authentic Voice

Finding your voice isn't about learning new techniques or following someone else's script for assertiveness. It's about uncovering and expressing the voice that's already within you—the voice that knows what you value, what you need, and what you're willing to stand for. This voice doesn't need to be manufactured or performed; it needs to be discovered and honored.

Your authentic voice is like a spring of water deep underground. It's always there, always flowing, but it needs the right conditions to reach the surface. Those conditions are created through the inner work of self-discovery, self-acceptance, and self-responsibility. When you've done this work, your voice doesn't need to be forced—it emerges naturally, like water finding its way to the surface.

This is why inspired action feels so different from forced action. Forced action is like trying to squeeze water from a stone—it requires enormous effort and produces minimal results. Inspired action is like removing the rocks that block a natural spring—once the obstacles are cleared, the water flows freely.

The research on intrinsic motivation supports this understanding. Studies consistently show that people are more likely to sustain behavior changes when those changes align with their core values and sense of identity. When action comes from external pressure or obligation, it requires constant willpower to maintain. When action comes from internal alignment and authentic commitment, it becomes self-sustaining.

This principle applies directly to finding your voice. When you try to speak up because you think you should, you're operating from external motivation. You might succeed for a while, but you'll eventually exhaust yourself and retreat to familiar patterns. When you speak up because staying silent would betray your authentic self, you're operating from intrinsic motivation. This type of action doesn't drain you—it energizes you because it expresses who you really are.

The beauty of inspired action is that it doesn't require you to become someone different. It requires you to become more fully yourself. You don't have to learn to be assertive—you have to learn to express your natural assertiveness. You don't have to develop confidence—you have to uncover the confidence that's already there but has been buried under layers of conditioning and fear.

The Price of Skipping Steps

When we try to change our behavior before changing our minds, we pay a significant price, both in the short term and the long term. The most immediate cost is exhaustion. Maintaining behavior that doesn't align with your inner reality requires constant energy and attention. It's like trying to hold a beach ball underwater—it takes enormous effort, and the moment you relax, it pops back to the surface.

I've seen this pattern repeatedly in my work with clients, friends, and relatives who've tried to transform their communication patterns through willpower alone. They might successfully speak up for a few weeks or even months, but eventually, they find themselves reverting to old patterns of silence. This isn't because they lack discipline or commitment—it's because they're trying to sustain behavior that doesn't feel natural or authentic.

The second cost is inconsistency. When your actions aren't rooted in genuine inner alignment, they become situational rather than reliable. You might speak up in low-stakes situations but retreat to silence when the pressure increases. You might be assertive with some people but passive with others. This inconsistency undermines both your credibility with others and your confidence in yourself.

The third cost is internal conflict. When there's a disconnect between your actions and your authentic self, you experience what psychologists call cognitive dissonance—the discomfort that comes from holding contradictory beliefs or behaviors. This internal conflict is exhausting and often leads to feelings of frustration, inadequacy, or confusion about who you really are.

Perhaps most significantly, skipping the inner work means missing the opportunity for genuine transformation. When you focus only on changing your behavior, you're treating symptoms rather than causes. You might temporarily alter how you respond to specific situations, but you don't address the underlying patterns that created those responses in the first place.

This is why so many people find themselves stuck in cycles of temporary change followed by regression. They make progress, hit a setback, and then feel like they're back to square one. But they're not actually back to square one: They've returned to their true starting point, a place they never fully left because they hadn't yet done the inner work to grow beyond it. We all start in different places.

The alternative is to invest in the inner work first. When you understand your authentic self, own your voice, and take the wheel of your life, external changes become natural expressions of internal transformation. You don't have to maintain your new behavior because it's not new—it's the authentic expression of who you've always been underneath the conditioning and fear.

The Connection to Purpose

Everything we've discussed about inspired action supports the central claim of this book: ***Finding your voice isn't about learning to speak—it's about remembering who you are.*** When you try to speak up without first remembering who you are, you're essentially trying to use someone else's voice. It might work temporarily, but it will never feel natural or sustainable.

Your authentic voice is inseparable from your authentic self. You can't express one without accessing the other. This is why all the communication techniques in the world won't help you if you haven't first done the work of self-discovery and self-acceptance. You'll be trying to use sophisticated tools without understanding the purpose they're meant to serve.

When you remember who you are—your values, your worth, your unique perspective—your voice becomes not just a tool for communication but an expression of your very essence. Speaking up isn't something you do; it's something you are. It's not a skill you've learned; it's a capacity you've always possessed but may have forgotten how to access.

This remembering process is what transforms forced action into inspired action. Instead of trying to become someone who speaks up, you recognize that you already are someone who speaks up—you've just been temporarily disconnected from that part of yourself. This understanding completely changes how you approach challenging situations. Instead of asking, "How can I force myself to speak up?" you ask, "What's preventing me from expressing my authentic self in this situation?" Instead of trying to borrow confidence from external sources, you work to reconnect with the confidence that's already within you.

The shift from forced to inspired action is ultimately a shift from *performing* to *being*. When you perform assertiveness, you're always one step removed from your authentic self. When you express your authentic voice, you're fully present and fully yourself. This presence and authenticity are what give your words their power and make your actions sustainable over time.

The Ripple Effect of Authentic Action

When your actions flow from authentic alignment rather than external pressure, they create ripple effects that extend far beyond the immediate situation. Inspired action has a quality of presence and power that influences not just what you say, but how others receive and respond to your words.

People can sense the difference between confidence that's

performed and self-respect that's real. They can feel the difference between words that are authentic rather than those that are rehearsed. When you speak from your true self, you naturally invite others to do the same. Your authenticity becomes contagious, creating space for more honest and meaningful interactions.

This ripple effect is particularly powerful in family systems and workplace dynamics. When you stop performing and start being authentic, it disrupts the entire system in positive ways. People who were comfortable with your previous patterns may initially resist the change, but they ultimately benefit from interacting with someone who's fully present and genuine.

I've seen this transformation repeatedly in my mediation work. When one person in a conflict begins speaking from authentic alignment rather than defensive positioning, it often catalyzes a similar shift in the other person. Authenticity begets authenticity, just as performance begets performance.

The sustainability of this approach cannot be overstated. When your actions are rooted in authentic self-expression, they don't require maintenance or reinforcement from others. They're self-sustaining because they're expressions of who you really are. This creates a stable foundation for ongoing growth and development in how you use your voice.

The Integration of Inner and Outer Work

The most powerful transformation happens when inner work and outer action are integrated rather than sequential. While it's important to do the foundational work of self-discovery and self-acceptance, there comes a point where you must test your new understanding in real-world situations. This testing process provides feedback that deepens your self-knowledge and refines your authentic expression.

Think of it as a spiral rather than a straight line. You do some inner work, take some inspired action, learn from the results, do more inner work, take more action, and so on. Each cycle deepens your understanding and strengthens your capacity to express your authentic voice in increasingly challenging situations.

This integration is particularly important because your authentic voice isn't a fixed entity—it's a dynamic, evolving expression of who you are. As you grow and change, your voice grows and changes with you. The key is maintaining the connection between your inner reality and your outer expression so that your voice remains a genuine reflection of your authentic self.

The practice of inspired action also helps you distinguish between your authentic voice and the voices of conditioning, fear, or people-pleasing. When you pay attention to how different types of action feel in your body and soul, you develop an internal compass that guides you toward authentic expression and away from performance or people-pleasing.

Moving Forward with Confidence

As we close this exploration of living out loud, I want to emphasize that this isn't about becoming perfect or never struggling with self-expression. It's about developing a reliable relationship with your authentic voice so that speaking up becomes a natural expression of who you are rather than a forced performance of who you think you should be.

The journey from silence to living out loud is ultimately a

journey home to yourself. It's about removing the barriers that prevent your authentic voice from emerging and creating the conditions where that voice can be expressed freely and powerfully. This doesn't happen overnight, but it does happen when you commit to the process of remembering who you are and honoring that truth in your daily interactions.

When action flows from authenticity, it carries a different quality of power. It doesn't drain you—it energizes you. It doesn't feel like work—it feels like expression. It doesn't require constant maintenance—it sustains itself because it's rooted in who you really are. This understanding transforms every aspect of how you approach communication and relationships. Instead of trying to become someone who speaks up, you recognize that you *already are* someone who speaks up—you've just been temporarily disconnected from that part of yourself. The work is about reconnection, not just transformation.

In our next chapter, we'll explore the final step in this journey: learning to live loud and love fully. We'll discover how all the inner work and personal responsibility culminate in a way of being that honors both your authentic self and your connections with others. But first, take a moment to appreciate how far you've come in your journey toward finding your voice. The fact that you're reading these words means you're already on the path from silence to authentic expression.

Your voice is not something you need to develop—it's something you need to remember. And that remembering happens one inspired action at a time, one authentic moment at a time, one courageous choice at a time. Your voice is waiting for you to come home to it. The question is: are you ready to take the next step?

NEW ADVENTURES IN SPEAKING MY TRUTH

As I sit here writing this final chapter, I'm struck by how different my life looks now compared to where I started. At an age when many of my peers are settling into retirement, I'm launching my next adventure—working with clients to reclaim their voices.

It's fitting, really, because my own journey to finding my voice has been anything but linear. It's been a winding path through several different careers, each one teaching me something essential about the cost of silence and the power of speaking up.

But let me start at the beginning, because understanding where I came from is crucial to understanding why this book exists—and why the steps we've walked through together matter so much.

The Early Years: Learning to Stay Small

My journey with silence began long before I entered my first career. Like many women of my generation, I was raised with subtle but persistent messages about being agreeable, not making waves, and prioritizing harmony over authenticity. "Choose your battles," they said. "Let it go." "Don't rock the boat." These well-meaning pieces of advice became the foundation of my early relationship with my own voice—or rather, my relationship with keeping it quiet.

When I started my career in social work, fresh out of graduate school and eager to make a difference, I thought I had found my calling. I was working in one of the busiest psychiatric hospitals in the country, surrounded by crisis and complexity every single day. You'd think that environment would have forced me to speak up, to advocate fiercely for my patients. And in many ways, it did. But what I discovered was that I could be a powerful advocate for others while remaining surprisingly silent about my own needs, concerns, and professional boundaries.

I remember one particular incident that still makes me cringe. A senior psychiatrist had made a treatment decision that I knew wasn't in the best interest of a patient I'd been working with for weeks. I had insights into her history and trauma responses that could have informed better care. But when it came time to speak up in the team meeting, I froze. The spotlight effect was in full force—I was convinced everyone would scrutinize my every word, judge my competence, and question my authority. So I stayed silent, telling myself I was being respectful, being a team player.

That patient didn't get the care she needed, and I carried that weight for months. It was my first real lesson in how the cost of silence extends far beyond ourselves.

The Pattern Emerges: Wherever I Went, There I Was

What I didn't realize then was that this pattern would follow me through every career transition. Each time I thought I was moving toward something that would naturally give me a voice, I found new ways to silence myself.

In education, I learned to speak up for my students with fierce determination, but I struggled to advocate for myself in staff meetings. When budget cuts threatened programs I'd built, when administrators made decisions that undermined learning, when colleagues dismissed ideas I knew could transform our school community—I often found myself nodding along, swallowing my words, convincing myself that keeping the peace was more important than speaking my truth.

In the field of education, *"Go along to get along"* wasn't just a saying—it was the mantra. It shaped hallway conversations, staff meetings, and professional reputations. Making waves could brand you as difficult, and once that label stuck, it had a way of following you—across classrooms, schools, even entire districts. The message was clear: keep your head down, don't challenge the system, and you'll keep your job.

The irony wasn't lost on me. Here I was, teaching children to find their voices, to express themselves clearly and confidently, while I was demonstrating the opposite. I was showing them that adult women smile and stay quiet, even when they disagree.

When I transitioned to working in the prison system, I thought surely this environment would force me to be more assertive. And it did, in many ways. Working with inmates with serious mental illness, facilitating groups, providing individual therapy—this work demanded presence, authenticity, and clear boundaries. But even there, I found myself struggling with the institutional hierarchy, the unspoken rules about how much a social worker could challenge the system, and how much advocacy was "appropriate."

I remember a particularly difficult case where I knew an inmate was being denied services he desperately needed. I had all the documentation, the clinical justification, and the moral imperative to speak up. But the system was complex, the personalities involved were challenging, and the potential for professional backlash felt real. I found myself caught between my ethical obligations and my learned pattern of avoiding conflict.

Each career brought its own version of the same lesson: I could be incredibly effective at speaking up for others, but when it came to my own voice, my own needs, my own professional convictions—silence still felt safer.

The Turning Point: When Silence Became Unbearable

The real transformation began when I started facing a reality that many women my age confront: chronic illness. Suddenly, staying silent wasn't just professionally limiting—it was potentially life-threatening. When you're dealing with health challenges, you simply cannot afford to be quiet about your needs, your symptoms, your treatment preferences. The healthcare system demands that you speak up, advocate for yourself, and ask the hard questions.

But here's what I discovered: all those years of practicing silence had made it incredibly difficult to find my voice when I needed it most. In examining rooms, I found myself deferring to medical professionals even when my instincts told me something was wrong. I'd leave appointments kicking myself for not asking the questions I'd prepared, for not pushing back when recommendations didn't feel right.

It was during this period that I had what I can only describe as a moment of clarity. I was sitting in yet another specialist's office, having just agreed to a treatment plan that didn't sit right with me, when I realized: I had spent decades helping other people find their voices, advocate for themselves, speak their truth. I had built entire careers around empowering others to stand up, speak out, and claim their space. Yet here I was, a master's-level clinician, a certified mediator, an award-winning educator—and I was still struggling with the same patterns I'd been carrying since childhood. Even though I had also found myself in a caregiving role for my mother and learned to advocate for her, when it came to myself, I found myself struggling again to be heard.

That was my rock-bottom moment with silence. I realized that all my professional success, all my expertise in helping others, meant nothing if I couldn't help myself. I had to face the uncomfortable truth: I was an expert at speaking up for everyone except Sue.

The Real Work Begins: Putting the Pieces Together

What followed was the most humbling and transformative work of my life. I had to take everything I knew about psychology, human behavior, and personal change and apply it to my own deeply ingrained patterns. I had to examine why someone with my background and expertise still struggled with something as fundamental as speaking up.

This is where the journey you've taken through this book became my own journey. I had to start with understanding the epidemic of silence—not just as a professional observation, but as a personal reality. I had to face the psychology behind my own tendency to stay quiet, to examine my own triggers, to build my own confidence from the ground up.

The work wasn't linear. There were setbacks, moments when I reverted to old patterns, situations where I walked away frustrated with myself for not speaking up. But slowly, steadily, I began to see changes. The framework I was developing wasn't just theoretical—it was being tested in real-time, in my own life.

I started small. I began speaking up in low-stakes situations, practicing the techniques I was learning, and celebrating small wins. I worked on changing my internal dialogue, challenging the spotlight effect, and breaking free from learned helplessness. I practiced assertiveness in daily interactions, built new habits, and slowly rewired decades of conditioning.

The breakthrough came when I realized that finding my voice wasn't about becoming a different person—it was about becoming more fully myself. All those years of professional training, all that experience helping others, all that knowledge about human psychology and behavior—that was my voice. I wasn't trying to become someone else; I was trying to step into *what was real for me.*

The Integration: Becoming a Mediator

My journey toward mediation felt like a natural evolution

of this work. As a Registered Neutral in civil and domestic relations, I can help people navigate difficult conversations, stand steady in conflict, and find their way through disagreement. But what I bring to this work isn't just professional training—it's the lived experience of having walked through my own journey from silence to voice.

When I sit across from clients who are struggling to speak up, to advocate for themselves, to stand firm in difficult conversations, I understand their fear from the inside out. I know what it feels like to have your heart racing, your mind going blank, your voice catching in your throat. I know the shame that comes from walking away from a situation, wishing you'd said something different. I know the frustration of having the perfect response hours later, when it's too late to matter.

But I also know something else: it's possible to change. Not overnight, not without work, but genuinely possible. The techniques in this book aren't just theoretical frameworks—they're tools that have been tested in the real world, by someone who needed them as much as anyone.

Living with Chronic Illness: A Different Kind of Voice

Managing chronic illness has added another layer to my understanding of voice and advocacy. Living with a condition that requires ongoing medical care, treatment decisions, and lifestyle adjustments has taught me that speaking up isn't just about professional situations or personal relationships—it's about survival. I don't focus on the illness; I don't allow myself to go there. I push myself to continue to do, and to *live* with this issue. Notice the emphasis on *live*.

Chronic illness has a way of stripping away pretense. When you're dealing with symptoms, navigating insurance systems, and coordinating care between multiple providers, you simply cannot afford to be polite at the expense of your health. You have to learn to ask direct questions, challenge recommendations that don't feel right, and advocate for accommodations you need.

But here's what I've learned: chronic illness doesn't automatically give you a voice. In fact, the vulnerability that comes with illness can make speaking up feel even more risky. When you're dependent on healthcare providers, when you're already feeling fragile, when you're navigating systems that can feel impersonal and overwhelming—it's easy to default to gratitude and compliance rather than advocacy and assertiveness.

The skills I've developed through this journey—the ability to speak up in real-time, to advocate for myself clearly and directly, to maintain my boundaries even in difficult situations—haven't just been professionally valuable. They've been essential to my health and wellbeing. I'm proud to say that I've fully stepped into the role of empowered patient—and in the process, my doctor has adapted his communication style to meet me where I am. We communicate with mutual respect and curiosity. He's even learned how to engage me in a way that invites thoughtful dialogue and actively supports my sense of agency in making decisions about my care.

The Adventure Continues: Choosing Growth Over Comfort

As I write this, I'm preparing to launch what many would consider a whole new career. At an age when society expects me to slow down, to settle into a quieter phase of life, I'm choosing adventure. I'm choosing to work with women who are ready to reclaim their voices, to step into their power, to stop holding back.

This choice isn't despite my chronic illness—it's because of everything I've learned through managing it. Living with a chronic condition has taught me that life is too short and too precious to spend it staying small. It's taught me that speaking up isn't just about professional success or personal satisfaction—it's about living authentically, making a difference, and refusing to let circumstances define your possibilities.

The women I work with now are at their own crossroads. They're tired of staying silent, tired of swallowing their words, tired of walking away from situations wishing they'd spoken up. They're ready to do the work, to face the discomfort, to build the skills they need to find their voice.

Why the Order Matters: The Journey You've Taken

Throughout this book, we've walked through a specific sequence of understanding and skill-building. This order isn't arbitrary—it mirrors the journey I had to take myself, and it reflects what I've learned about how real change happens.

We started with understanding the epidemic of silence because you can't change what you don't acknowledge. I had to face the reality that staying quiet was a pattern, not just a series of isolated incidents. I had to understand that this wasn't a personal failing but a widespread challenge with identifiable roots.

We explored the psychology behind speaking up because

surface-level tips and techniques don't work when you're dealing with deeply ingrained patterns. I had to understand why my brain was wired to choose silence, why conflict felt so threatening, and why speaking up seemed so risky. Without this understanding, I was just fighting symptoms instead of addressing causes.

We worked on identifying triggers because you can't manage what you can't see coming. I had to develop awareness of the situations, people, and dynamics that activated my silent response. This awareness became the foundation for everything that followed.

We focused on building confidence because assertiveness without self-worth is just aggression. I had to do the internal work of believing that my voice mattered, that my opinions were valid, that I deserved to take up space. This wasn't about becoming someone else—it was about becoming more fully myself.

We practiced specific techniques because knowledge without application is just information. I had to actually use these tools in real situations, make mistakes, learn from them, and gradually build new habits. The techniques had to be tested and refined through practice.

We addressed obstacles because the journey isn't linear. I had to develop strategies for managing anxiety, handling negative reactions, and maintaining my progress even when it felt difficult. Real change requires sustainability, not just initial success.

This sequence mattered because each step built on the previous ones. You can't skip to the techniques without understanding why you need them. You can't build confidence without acknowledging the patterns that undermined it. You can't practice assertiveness without recognizing what triggers your silence.

The Transformation: Who I Am Now

So what does the "other side" look like? What has changed, and what does finding my voice actually mean in daily life?

I wish I could tell you that I never struggle with speaking up anymore, that I've completely overcome decades of conditioning. That wouldn't be true, and it wouldn't be helpful. What I can tell you is that my relationship with my voice has fundamentally changed.

I no longer default to silence. When I'm in a situation where I need to speak up, my first instinct isn't to avoid or defer. I might still feel the weight of the moment. I've learned to recognize my triggers in real-time. When I feel that familiar tightness in my chest, when I notice my thoughts racing or my voice starting to catch, I know what's happening. I can **pause, breathe, and choose my response** rather than just reacting from old patterns, and either responding ineffectively or shrinking into silence.

I've developed what I call "voice recovery time"—the ability to speak up even when I didn't initially. If I walk away from a situation having stayed quiet when I should have spoken up, I don't just carry that frustration indefinitely. I reach out, I follow up, I find a way to say what needs to be said. It might not be in the moment, but it's not lost forever.

Most importantly, I've learned to trust myself. I trust my instincts, my expertise, my right to take up space. This isn't about being aggressive or confrontational—it's about being authentic. It's about showing up as myself, with all my knowledge and experience, and opinions, rather than as a smaller, quieter version of myself.

The Ripple Effect: Beyond Personal Change

Finding my voice has changed more than just my ability to speak up in difficult situations. It's transformed how I show up in all areas of my life.

In my relationships, I'm more honest about my needs and boundaries. I can disagree without fear of losing connection. I can ask for what I need without apologizing for having needs in the first place.

In my professional life, I bring my full expertise to every interaction. I share my insights, challenge ideas when necessary, and advocate for approaches I believe in. I've learned that my experience and knowledge are valuable contributions, not impositions.

In managing my health, I'm an active partner in my care. I ask thoughtful questions, seek additional opinions when necessary, and advocate for treatments that align with my values and goals. I've come to understand that being a "good patient" isn't about acceptance and passivity—it's about staying informed, engaged, and empowered.

The Work Continues: Why I Do What I Do

This journey has led me to my current work with women who are ready to reclaim their voices. In this new endeavor, I have the privilege of working with incredible women who are tired of staying small, tired of swallowing their words, and tired of walking away from situations wishing they'd spoken up.

What I bring to this work isn't just professional training—it's the lived experience of having walked this path myself. I know what it feels like to struggle with speaking up despite having all the "right" credentials and experience. I know what it's like to be an expert at advocating for others while struggling to advocate for yourself.

But I also know what's possible. I know that the patterns we've carried for decades can be changed. I know that finding your voice isn't about becoming someone else—it's about becoming more fully yourself. I know that the journey is worth it, even when it's uncomfortable, even when it's hard.

The Adventure Mindset: Embracing What's Next

As I look ahead, I'm filled with excitement rather than anxiety. This mindset shift—from fear of the unknown to excitement about possibilities—is perhaps the most profound change of all.

Living with chronic illness has taught me that life is unpredictable, that plans can change, and that adaptability is essential. But it's also taught me that limitations don't have to define possibilities. Finding my voice has given me the tools to navigate uncertainty, to advocate for what I need, to create the life I want rather than just accepting what feels safe.

My new clients often start our conversations by telling me what they can't do, what they're afraid of, what's holding them back. By the end of our work together, they're talking about what they want to create, what they're excited to try, what's possible when they stop letting fear make their decisions.

This shift—from limitation to possibility, from fear to excitement, from silence to voice—is at the heart of why this work matters so much.

Coming Full Circle: The Gift of the Journey

As I finish writing this book, I'm struck by how perfectly the journey has come full circle. I started my career wanting to help people, to make a difference, to use my voice in service of others. Along the way, I learned that I couldn't fully help others find their voices until I had found my own.

The techniques in this book, the framework we've explored together, the steps we've taken—these aren't just professional tools I've developed. They're personal practices that have transformed my life. They've taken me from someone who knew how to help others speak up but struggled to speak up herself, to someone who can model what it looks like to live with voice and authenticity.

The journey hasn't been easy. There have been moments of discomfort, setbacks, and situations where I've had to practice these skills in real-time. But every challenge has reinforced the same truth: Finding your voice isn't a destination you reach once and then you're done. It's an ongoing practice, a daily choice, a way of being in the world.

Your Journey: What's Possible

If you've made it through this book, if you've done the work, if you've started practicing these skills, then you're already on your way. You might not feel dramatically different yet—transformation takes time. But you've planted seeds that will continue to grow.

The most important thing I can tell you is this: you don't have to wait until you feel completely confident to start speaking up. You don't have to master every technique before you use your voice. You don't have to overcome every fear before you take action.

The famous quote attributed to Arthur Ashe never gets old: *Start where you are. Use what you have. Do what you can.* Your voice matters—not someday when you're more prepared, not eventually when you're more confident, but right now, as you are.

The world needs what you have to offer. Your insights, your experience, your perspective—these are gifts that can only be shared when you're willing to speak up. The women and men in your life need to see what it looks like to live with voice and authenticity. The challenges in your workplace, your community, your relationships—these need people who are willing to speak up, even when it's uncomfortable.

You have everything you need to begin. The techniques are in your hands. The understanding is in your mind. The courage is in your heart.

The only question left is: What will you do with your voice?

Your adventure is just beginning.

ABOUT THE AUTHOR

Sue Levine is a Licensed Clinical Social Worker, retired educator, Registered Neutral (mediator), and National Board Certified Health and Wellness Coach with a long-standing passion for helping people find their voices and live with intention. Her journey has taken her through some of the most complex corners of the human experience: from working in one of the busiest psychiatric hospitals in the country, supporting individuals in crisis, to leading classrooms and designing inclusive learning environments.

Recently, she worked in a prison setting, supporting inmates with serious mental illness by facilitating groups and providing individual therapy—a role that deepened her understanding of resilience, hope, and the power of compassionate connection. These experiences continue to influence how she has come to view healing and personal strength.

Her early career in social work included working with patients facing acute psychosis, substance use disorders, and complex forensic cases—experiences that deeply shaped her belief in the resilience of the human spirit. She later transitioned into education, serving as a classroom teacher, reading specialist, and ultimately as a Teacher-Librarian. In 2014, she was honored as Teacher-Librarian of the Year in a large metro area school district—a role that allowed her to champion literacy, inclusion, and innovation at the heart of the school community.

During her years in education, Sue reimagined an antiquated district science center library (with microfilm and century-old books with outdated information) into a vibrant community space, and innovated an award-winning preschool STEM program that introduced young learners to science through joyful, hands-on experiences. She is proud to have earned National Board Teacher Certification in Reading in 2006 and to have been granted a Fulbright Distinguished Teacher Award to carry out an inquiry project in New Zealand on creating inclusive libraries that reflect cultural and disability diversity in 2016.

Sue has always been drawn to the power of words, clarity, and connection. Last year, she became a Registered Neutral (mediator) in Civil and Domestic Relations, further expanding her work in helping people navigate difficult conversations and stand steady in the face of conflict.

Academically, Sue holds a BA in Psychology, a Master of Social Work, a Master of Public Administration, a Master of Technical and Professional Communication, an Educational Specialist degree, and a TESOL certificate. Each path has shaped how she thinks, listens, and helps others navigate meaningful change.

Now, as a National Board Certified Health and Wellness Coach, Sue plans to work with women who are ready to stop holding back and start speaking up—especially in those real-time moments when silence has become the default. *Speak Up! It's Your Life* was born from the understanding that finding your voice isn't just about learning to speak—it's about remembering who you are.

When Sue is not writing, reflecting, or exploring new ways to support others, you'll find her enjoying quiet time—or chatting on the phone with friends and family, where some of the best connections happen. She also loves jumping on the rebounder; it's playful, energizing, and a reminder that movement doesn't have to be serious to be good for the soul. Sue enjoys finding creative ways to make everyday meals more nourishing—like experimenting with ingredient swaps and growing her own microgreens on the kitchen counter under grow lights.

Sue believes that change doesn't come from pressure—it comes from clarity, readiness, and the decision to begin.

ACKNOWLEDGMENTS

To my late father, who always listened to me with patience and care. Even before I found my own voice, your steady presence and unwavering support gave me comfort and courage. I carry your love with me every day.

To my sister-in-law, Elissa, this project has been a long road, and you've been with me every step of the way. Thank you for helping me recall stories I thought I'd forgotten and for spending so much time helping me sort through my thoughts. The kindness, clarity, and commitment you showed helped carry me through this entire process, and for that, I am forever grateful.

To Karen, my in-house grammarian and word wrangler extraordinaire. You spot the sneaky typos, tame the unruly sentences, and somehow make grammar both heroic and hilarious. I don't know how I ever wrote a sentence without you, thank you!

To my nephew Eric, who's all grown up now and still believes his old aunt can take on new projects like she's 25. Thank you for always cheering me on, nudging me forward, and reminding me that it's never too late to start a new adventure. Your encouragement and endless support mean more than you know.

To my lifelong childhood friend Mona, you always spoke up, even when we were young. Back then, I didn't yet know how to find my voice, but you showed me what it looked like. You always stood up for what was right. Your courage and honesty inspired me then—and continue to inspire me today. I especially want to thank you for speaking up for me on that difficult day in high school, when you set that teacher straight on my behalf. You were (and still are) an incredible friend and advocate, and I'm forever grateful.

To my friend Sandy, an avid reader and creative collaborator—thank you for being a wonderful sounding board and for all the idea-filled conversations about projects and possibilities, thanks for the laughter!

To the friends and coworkers who courageously shared their struggles with speaking up—your honesty and vulnerability inspired me more than you know.

To all of my Facebook friends, thank you for always encouraging me to write a book. Your support, comments, and belief in my voice helped make this possible. I'm truly grateful for the encouragement and kindness you've shared along the way.

To my publishing team, led by Lin Eleoff at AFGO Press—thank you for your patience, flexibility, and steadfast support throughout this journey. Your belief in this project helped bring the book to life exactly as it was meant to be. A special shout-out to the project's editor, Kate, whose keen eye, thoughtful feedback, and generous spirit shaped this manuscript into its best self. Your presence throughout this process has meant more than I can say.

To Thomas Gonzalez of Tomprints, the creative mind behind the cover art, whose talent and vision brought this book's first impression to life—my heartfelt thanks!

This book would not have been possible without the incredible women who have inspired me throughout my journey—those who have bravely spoken up, stood firm, and shown me the true power of finding one's voice. To every woman who has felt unheard or overlooked but still dared to speak her truth—this book is for you.

Lastly, to the women whose voices have been silenced by culture, fear, or violence—you are seen, your struggles are real, and your strength is profound. Though speaking up may not always be possible, your courage lives in every quiet act of resilience. This book holds space for you and honors the bravery it takes to endure and survive.

IS IT TIME TO FIND YOUR VOICE?

Take this short quiz to reflect on where you are and whether you're ready to take the first steps toward speaking up, standing firm, and honoring your truth.

1. Do you often find yourself replaying conversations, thinking about what you should have said?

- ☐ Never
- ☐ Occasionally
- ☐ Frequently
- ☐ Almost Always

2. When someone says or does something that makes you uncomfortable, do you speak up?

- ☐ Never
- ☐ Occasionally
- ☐ Frequently
- ☐ Almost Always

3. Do you worry that advocating for your needs will be seen as "too much" or "selfish"?

- ☐ Never
- ☐ Occasionally
- ☐ Frequently
- ☐ Almost Always

4. Have you ever said "yes" when you truly wanted to say "no"?

- ☐ Never
- ☐ Occasionally
- ☐ Frequently
- ☐ Almost Always

5. Do you hesitate to express your opinion in group settings—even when you know you're right?

- ☐ Never
- ☐ Occasionally
- ☐ Frequently
- ☐ Almost Always

6. Are you more concerned with keeping the peace than being honest?

- ☐ Never
- ☐ Occasionally
- ☐ Frequently

- ☐ Almost Always

7. Do you tend to minimize your feelings, needs, or discomfort in relationships?

- ☐ Never
- ☐ Occasionally
- ☐ Frequently
- ☐ Almost Always

8. Do you struggle to make decisions without second-guessing yourself?

- ☐ Never
- ☐ Occasionally
- ☐ Frequently
- ☐ Almost Always

9. Have you stopped speaking up because you've been dismissed, ignored, or punished for it in the past?

- ☐ Never
- ☐ Occasionally
- ☐ Frequently
- ☐ Almost Always

10. Do you ever feel invisible in conversations, meetings, or relationships?

- ☐ Never
- ☐ Occasionally

- Frequently
- Almost Always

11. When something isn't right, do you tell yourself "it's not worth it" to say anything?

- Never
- Occasionally
- Frequently
- Almost Always

12. Do you feel emotionally drained after interactions where you didn't speak your truth?

- Never
- Occasionally
- Frequently
- Almost Always

13. Do you silence yourself because you don't want to be labeled as difficult, dramatic, or emotional?

- Never
- Occasionally
- Frequently
- Almost Always

14. Are you aware of what keeps you silent, even when you want to speak?

- Never

- ☐ Occasionally
- ☐ Frequently
- ☐ Almost Always

15. Do you feel ready—even just a little—to explore what life could be like if you spoke up more often?

- ☐ Never
- ☐ Occasionally
- ☐ Frequently
- ☐ Almost Always

What Your Score Means

Mostly "Always" or "Almost Always"

You've likely been quiet for too long—and it's wearing on you. Whether it's guilt, fear, or habit, something is keeping you from honoring your truth. You may feel invisible or resentful. The good news? You're aware of it now. That's your starting line.

Mostly "Sometimes" or "Occasionally"

You're on the fence—aware of when you silence yourself, but still struggling to speak up consistently. You're not stuck—you're in transition. With the right support and tools, you can start turning hesitation into clarity and confidence.

Mostly "Never"

You may already feel strong in your voice and know how to advocate for yourself—beautiful. Or… you may be so used to pushing things down that you no longer notice the silence. Take a moment to reflect: are you being honest with yourself about how you really feel and what you really need?

Hey, Look at You—Finishing the Book!

That's no small thing. As a little thank-you (and a gentle nudge to keep the momentum going), I've got a free gift for you: the **Personal Change Workbook**. It's an easy-to-use, no-pressure companion full of thoughtful prompts and simple tools to help you keep moving forward—your way, on your terms.

Grab your copy at suelevine.com. Just pop in your email, confirm, and it'll be on its way to your inbox. You'll also get occasional notes from me with ideas, inspiration, and reminders that you've got this.

Start where you are—one step is all it takes!

Thank you for your interest in

SPEAK UP!
IT'S YOUR LIFE

By Sue Levine, LCSW, NBC-HWC

Published by AFGO Press

AFGO Press is a division of AFGO Media and Publishing, whose mission is to support women in building their own businesses.

For more information, go to
AFGOmedia.com

www.ingramcontent.com/pod-product-compliance
Lightning Source LLC
Chambersburg PA
CBHW071135090426
42736CB00012B/2127